Which Test cricketer's
What is Ian Botham's
Who once scored 180 b
Who wrote *Beyond a I*

With these and 416 other
puzzle, entertain and inf
strand of cricket's rich tapestry, and the book is full of wit
and humour as well as facts. Derek Lodge, having won the
Council of Cricket Societies quiz three years running, was
promoted to setting it. He is also the author of the acclaimed
Figures on the Green.

DEREK LODGE
A QUESTION OF CRICKET

London
UNWIN PAPERBACKS
Boston   Sydney

First published in Great Britain by Unwin Paperbacks 1983

UNWIN® PAPERBACKS
40 Museum Street, London WC1A 1LU, UK

Unwin Paperbacks
Park Lane, Hemel Hempstead, Herts HP2 4TE, UK

George Allen & Unwin Australia Pty Ltd
8 Napier Street, North Sydney, NSW 2060, Australia

To R.W.
    T.R.T.
    F.G.P.
    who have answered questions I haven't asked, and asked
    questions I couldn't answer.

British Library Cataloguing in Publication Data

Lodge, Derek
    A question of cricket
1.   Cricket—Miscellanea
I.   Title
796.35′8′076   GV917
ISBN 0-04-79607-01

Set in 10 on 11 point Times by V & M Graphics Ltd, Aylesbury, Bucks
and printed in Great Britain
by Cox and Wyman Ltd, Reading

Preface

I have been setting quizzes for some years now, and I was delighted when John Newth gave me the opportunity to put a few questions in book form. There are really three types of quiz. First, those in which the questions are put across the table and have to be answered within a time-limit. In general, when one is setting this type of question, it is as well to aim at a reasonably high success rate for the competitors – between, say, 50% and 70%. Otherwise the quiz can be embarrassing for the participants and rather tedious for the audience. However, it is not always easy to determine the success rate in advance; some contestants are amazingly expert. Last year, I asked the participants in the Council of Cricket Societies quiz to name the 17 county captains in 1946, and I was not a little surprised when one of them got all 17 and another (the ultimate winner) 15. When the competition is as hot as this, the quizmaster has a few problems.

The second type of quiz is the written quiz which requires the reader to answer without an inordinate amount of research, but not under time-pressure. The questions can be a little more difficult than in oral quizzes, but the questioner does not feel that his ingenuity is impossibly stretched. Finally comes the prize quiz, where entrants have to hunt for the answers in slow time, making full use of works of reference. I find this type of quiz very difficult indeed to set. One does not want every question to be capable of being answered from the standard works, or everybody gets it right; on the other hand, it would be unfair to set the questions in such a way that only those with access to really massive libraries can cope with them. A judicious mixture of the straight question and the conundrum helps, but it is desperately difficult to avoid ambiguity.

The questions in this book are designed to be answered either orally, if friends choose to get together and put each other's knowledge to the test, or in the arm chair, train or aeroplane if readers want to try them on their own. But I suggest that the greatest fun will be had by those who play the game honestly, trying first to answer without reference books, then looking the answers up in books, and only referring to the answer pages when baffled. I have tried to make these answer pages interesting by including a good deal more information than is strictly necessary. If I have succeeded in giving both information and amusement, I shall have achieved my purpose.

The reader should be aware that the information is up-to-date to the end of the 1982 English season and does not include the events of the 1982–83 seasons in Pakistan, Australia and elsewhere.

A list of useful reference books to which I have had recourse may be of interest:

Bill Frindall, *Wisden Book of Test Cricket*
Bill Frindall, *Wisden Book of Cricket Records*
James Gibb, *Test Cricket Records*
Christopher Martin-Jenkins, *The Complete Who's Who of Test Cricketers*
B. J. Wakley, *Classic Centuries*
Wisden Cricketers' Almanack, all years

I am immensely grateful to Howard Milton, Tony Thorpe and Robby Wilton for looking over the questions and answers in search of errors and ambiguities; if any such remain, they are my responsibility.

DEREK LODGE

Note: The picture quiz will be found in the centre of the book, between pages 64 and 65. The answers to it are at the end of the answers section.

1. The 1982 season

Whenever I set quizzes, the immediate past always proves more difficult to the contestants than earlier times. I am not sure why, but it may be that we learn about the summer's events as they happen, and then reinforce our learning by reading the next year's *Wisden* and other books. Anyway, it happens, and so I have not made this set of questions too difficult.

1. Which batsman was the first to complete 1000 runs in first-class cricket?

2. Which wicket-keeper was the first to make 50 dismissals?

3. Who scored his tenth Test century during the season?

4. A county played a first-class home match outside the county, on a ground in the middle of a racecourse. Which county, which ground?

5. Who was the Pakistani umpire who 'stood' in first-class matches during the season?

6. Which Pakistani bowler was sent for from Pakistan, as distinct from being called up from League cricket, to reinforce the touring team?

7. Who was twice left not out in the nineties in the same match, by his captain's declarations?

8. Which batsman was run out when batting with a runner, although his runner had made good his ground?

9. Who was the top Englishman in the first-class bowling averages?

10. Who scored his maiden century, failing by only one run to help equal his county's record for the last wicket, and achieved his best-ever bowling performance in the same match?

2. England v. Australia, 1877-1938

1. When did seven men score centuries in the same Test, and who were they?

2. When did six men from one county play together for England?

3. Australia made 11 changes between the first and second Tests of 1884-85. Why?

4. Which two fast bowlers each took ten wickets in their first Test?

5. Who made four hundreds in five successive innings which he played on one ground?

6. In which series did the two captains share the same birthday?

7. What was the highest score between 1877 and 1938 by a captain in an England v. Australia Test?

8. A Test has been won and lost before lunch on the second day – true or false?

9. Until Don Bradman overtook him, Jack Hobbs held the record for the highest aggregate in England v. Australia Tests. Whom did *he* overtake?

10. When was the first Timeless Test played in England?

3. England v. Australia, 1946-81

1. Who was the first England captain to put Australia in in this period, and what happened?

2. And who was the first England captain after 1946 to score a century in Australia?

3. Who took 5 for 28 in the first Test innings in which he bowled?

4. Who played in his only Test because Lindwall had chickenpox?

5. Who played the longest first-class innings made in Australia?

6. Who scored ten consecutive first-class fifties at Adelaide?

7. In which Test did the two wicket-keepers dismiss 16 batsmen between them?

8. When did 20 wickets fall in a day which began after lunch?

9. Which two players have batted on all five days of a Test?

10. Which is the longest match ever played in England?

4. England v. South Africa

1. Who took 26 wickets in his first and only Test series?

2. Who took 6 for 200 at the Oval in his only Test?

3. Name four Australians who played for England against South Africa, and also played for Australia.

4. Who took most wickets, for either side, in England v. South Africa Tests?

5. Which Yorkshireman was called from his garden on the morning of the match to play against South Africa, and distinguished himself?

6. Who was summoned to join a South African touring side while on holiday?

7. Who was the youngest man to score a century for South Africa against England?

8. On how many grounds have Tests been played between the two countries?

9. Who took most wickets in a Test for South Africa against any country?

10. One country has been represented by the same XI in each match of a five-match series – true or false?

5. England v. West Indies

1. Have two West Indian brothers ever scored fifties in the same Test against England?

2. When did one side score more by way of extras in a match than the runs contributed by any one batsman?

3. When was the last time England had two wins in a series against the West Indies?

4. In which match did one side aggregate over 1000 runs?

5. What is the record number of runs to be added for the last three wickets (in aggregate) in a Test?

6. When was the last time in any Test that three men scored centuries in the same innings?

7. When did a side reach 330 for 2 by teatime on the first day, yet come within measurable distance of defeat?

8. Who scored 137 in his second and last Test?

9. When did two cousins save the West Indies with a massive sixth-wicket stand?

10. Which captain lost a Test after declaring with two wickets down?

6. English Test cricketers

1. Which three men made their *first-class* debuts in the same Test series?

2. Who batted in over 100 Test innings, but only twice went in in any position other than no. 1 or no. 2?

3. Who scored the first 200 for England in England?

4. Who scored most boundaries in a Test innings?

5. Who scored 62 out of 103 all out at Melbourne?

6. Who scored most runs before lunch in a Test?

7. Which England player was the first to die?

8. And which was born at the earliest date (in 1827, in fact)?

9. Who played for England in just one Test, in which he neither batted nor bowled?

10. Name the 19 men who played for England both before and after the second world war.

7. Australian Test cricketers

1. Who was the first Australian to umpire in a Test match and *later* to play in one?

2. Arthur Mailey once took ten for 66, as is quite well-known, but which other Australian cricketer did so (not in a Test)?

3. Who played in one Test, in Australia, but played in first-class matches on three separate tours of England?

4. Sobers and Gibbs are the most successful fielder/bowler combination in all Test cricket, but who are the most successful Australian combination?

5. Who is said to have refused to captain Australia on tour unless his brother was also selected?

6. Who toured England on eight tours on which Tests were played?

7. Who did the hat-trick in his last Test?

8. Who was the last wicket-keeper to captain Australia?

9. Four bowlers were accused of throwing in the same post-war series. Who were they?

10. Who took 5 for 37 in his first Test, in which he had replaced his injured captain?

8. South African Test cricketers

1. Two South Africans each made two centuries in a Test, in the same series. Who were they?

2. Who scored three Test centuries for South Africa before he was 21?

3. Who was 'the terrible Greek' and what did he do?

4. Who was the last man to play cricket for South Africa and rugby for England?

5. Who captained South Africa in his only Test and bowled Victor Trumper in it?

6. Who made the record Test partnership for South Africa?

7. Who were the four googly bowlers in the 1907 touring team?

8. Who scored most runs for South Africa in a Test series?

9. Who captained South Africa in ten Tests and won none of them?

10. Who did the double while on tour in England?

9. West Indian Test cricketers

1. In 1929–30, the West Indies had four different captains in the four Tests. Why was this, and who were they?

2. In one Test between the West Indies and Australia, four players made their maiden Test centuries. When did this happen, who were the four players, and was there any special reason why it happened?

3. What is the highest individual score for West Indies against Australia, and what other record was set in the same innings?

4. West Indies have never made a tenth-wicket stand of over 100 in a Test – true or false?

5. Which West Indian Test players had the Christian names of Hammond, Simpson and McDonald?

6. Who took nine wickets for the West Indies in the tied Test?

7. Who made the first Test century for the West Indies?

8. Which West Indian Test player appeared for Oxford at the age of 39?

9. Who scored three successive Test centuries for West Indies in 1976?

10. When did the West Indies draw all five Tests of a rubber?

10. New Zealand Test cricketers

1. Which New Zealander scored the highest percentage of runs in any completed first-class innings?

2. Who took a wicket with his first ball in his only Test?

3. Of which New Zealand bowler did *Wisden* say: 'Had he been an Australian he might have been termed a wonder of the age'?

4. Which New Zealand Test player was born in India?

5. Who took a hat-trick in his first Test for New Zealand?

6. And who, in his first Test, scored a century and took five wickets in an innings?

7. Which New Zealander bowled two successive overs in a Test innings?

8. Which New Zealand Test cricketer died of wounds sustained in the second world war?

9. Who dismissed Boycott six times in Tests?

10. Which father and son both played for New Zealand before they were 21?

11. Indian Test cricketers

1. Who scored a century in the second innings of three successive Tests, but only made seven runs in all in the first innings of those Tests?

2. Who scored a Test fifty in under half an hour?

3. Which Indian Test captain had a son who played in the Test series of 1981–82?

4. Who scored 99 in 500 minutes in a Test?

5. Who scored the first 200 for India in a Test?

6. Who was dismissed for a 'pair' four times in Tests?

7. Which opening batsman was out for a duck five times in one series?

8. Who has taken most Test wickets for India, and how many has he taken?

9. What is the record Test partnership for India for any wicket?

10. Who is the youngest man to have played Test cricket for India?

12. Pakistani Test cricketers

1. Who is the oldest player to have appeared for Pakistan?

2. Which three Pakistani Test players have also played in Tests for another country?

3. What is the record Test partnership for Pakistan for any wicket?

4. Which player scored a double-century and took five wickets in an innings for Pakistan in the same Test?

5. Who were the father and son who both played famous long, slow innings for Pakistan?

6. Who captained Pakistan when they first beat Australia?

7. Who has scored a hundred before lunch on the first day of a Test for Pakistan?

8. Whose only Test century for Pakistan was a double-century?

9. Who took almost half the wickets for Pakistan in their first Test series against England?

10. Who has made two double-centuries for Pakistan against England, and when did he do so?

13. Australia v. West Indies

1. Who made the highest score in the tied Test at Brisbane in 1960?

2. Which batsman was run out by which bowler while backing up in a Test?

3. Who has taken most wickets in a Test for West Indies in Australia?

4. Australia's opening bowlers both made centuries in the same Test in 1955. Who were they?

5. One of the captains in the very first Test played between the two countries scored a not-out fifty in each innings. Who was he?

6. When did a Test selector have to umpire a Test, and who was he?

7. Roy Fredericks made the fastest century by a West Indian batsman, in terms of balls bowled to him. How many?

8. In 1979–80, an Australian batsman made more runs on his Test debut than any other player has done without scoring a century. Who was he, and how many did he score?

9. Who scored six fifties in successive Test innings in 1968–69?

10. Which West Indian wicket-keeper scored his only first-class century in a Test against Australia?

14. Youth

This quiz is about players who distinguished themselves at a relatively early age, mostly, but not all, in Test cricket.

1. Who scored most Test centuries before his twenty-first birthday?

2. And who took most Test wickets before he was 21?

3. Who is the only cricketer to have captained a Test team of which all the other ten were older than himself?

4. Who is the youngest man to have captained England?

5. Who are the youngest pair to have opened the batting for England (that is, the pair whose combined ages were the lowest)?

6. Who played in a first-class match in 1914, at the age of 15, and also played first-class cricket after the end of the second world war?

7. Who is the youngest man to have scored a Test century for England?

8. And the youngest to do so for Australia?

9. Which two contemporary players appeared for England before their twenty-first birthdays?

10. In the third 'Victory Test' of 1945. three 18-year-olds appeared for the England team. Two of them were subsequently selected for full Test sides. Who were the three?

15. Age

To redress the balance, a set of questions about players who distinguished themselves late in their cricketing lives.

1. Who is the oldest man to have scored a Test century?

2. Which father and son played for their country after they were 40?

3. Who had the longest Test career, in the sense of the time which elapsed between his first Test appearance and his last?

4. Who played in an English first-class match after he was 60?

5. Who is the oldest man to have scored 300 in a Test innings?

6. And the oldest to do so in a first-class match?

7. Who took most wickets in a Test played after his fortieth birthday?

8. Which two Australians played in Tests after the second world war when over the age of 40?

9. When did three men over 40 score centuries in the same series played between England and Australia?

10. Who was the last man to play first-class cricket in five decades?

16. The numbers game (part 1)

When I set cricket quizzes 'face to face', one of the most dreaded rounds is the one in which I reverse the usual order of questioning and, instead of asking, say, for the highest score made in a Test by a Pakistani batsman, I put the number 274 before the victim and invite him (or her, but it's usually a him) to say what feat the number suggests. People are remarkably thrown by having the question this way round. In tackling the numbers below, the reader should remember that the figure represents a feat which either is a record, or was one at the time. Thus, if I ask for the meaning of 304, I shall be looking for Freeman's victims in a season and not for Bradman's score in a Test, which wasn't even the Leeds record.

1. 365.
2. 577.
3. 424.
4. 46.
5. 4187.

6. 6996.
7. 774.
8. 287.
9. 1294.
10. 151.

17. The numbers game (part 2)

1. 499.
2. 49.
3. 309.
4. 974.
5. 451.

6. 3816.
7. 561.
8. 8114.
9. 78.
10. 1690.

18. Grounds

This round contains some general questions about the grounds on which first-class cricket is, or has been played.

1. On which three grounds in Bombay has Test cricket been played?

2. Which is the latest city in India to stage a Test for the first time?

3. Where is the Test ground named St George's Park?

4. To the end of the English season of 1980, 49 first-class matches had been concluded in a single day. 22 of these were played on one ground. Which ground?

5. Which county has its headquarters at Nottingham Road?

6. And which has a county ground at Clarence Park?

7. On which Test ground is the Vulture Street end?

8. Which county plays on Courtauld's ground?

9. And which on May's Bounty?

10. In which town were both Castle Park and the Garrison ground, both being first-class grounds?

19. Fifty years ago

A quiz for the older reader. Fifty years before the publication date of this book, there was played in Australia one of the most famous Test series of all time, the so-called 'bodyline' series. The first five questions below concern that Australian season, the second five the English season of 1933, when the West Indies toured England for their second Test-playing tour.

1. By a curious coincidence, two England batsmen scored precisely the same number of runs in the 1932–33 series, and at the same average. Who were they, and how many did they score?

2. Who made the highest individual score for Australia in the series?

3. Who scored a hundred for England on his first appearance in a Test?

4. What did E. Paynter do in the fourth Test, at Brisbane?

5. Who took ten wickets in an innings in a Sheffield Shield match in that season?

6. Who was top of the West Indian batting averages on the 1933 tour?

7. And who was top of the English first-class batting averages, scoring 3323 runs?

8. Why were there no Minor Counties Champions in 1933?

9. Two men who played for Middlesex that year played in Test cricket after the second world war. Who were they?

10. Which two West Indies bowlers bowled bodyline in the Old Trafford Test?

20.   Nicknames

Room for twenty questions on this page, since there is not a great deal to say about a nickname (although I have tried to offer explanations of the names on the answer pages, where they are obscure or particularly interesting). Who, then, bore these nicknames?

1. The Croucher.
2. Hopper (two players).
3. The Essex Treasure.
4. Father.
5. Ollie.
6. Noddy.
7. Chilly.
8. Stalky (two players).
9. Dodger.
10. The Coroner.
11. Horseshoe.
12. The Big Ship.
13. Dainty.
14. Mother.
15. The Governor-General.
16. Rowdy.
17. Napper.
18. Musso.
19. Froggy.
20. Tiger (*five* players).

21. Figures

A real test for the statistical addicts. I give in some detail the Test career figures of ten players, all of whom have, or appear to have, finished their Test careers. Can you name them?

1. 3612 runs, ave. 46.30, highest score 262 not out.

2. 3631 runs, ave. 42.22, highest score 223. 35 wickets, ave. 42.14.

3. 3208 runs, ave. 39.12, highest score 189 not out. 1 wicket for 44.

4. 2727 runs, ave. 40.10, highest score 230 not out. 4 wickets, ave. 86.00.

5. 2516 runs, ave. 45.74, highest score 201. 40 wickets, ave. 34.05.

6. 4334 runs, ave. 42.49, highest score 169. 7 wickets, ave. 78.28.

7. 2440 runs, ave. 42.06, highest score 255 not out. 0 wickets.

8. 4737 runs, ave. 43.45, highest score 171. 0 wickets.

9. 2131 runs, ave. 41.78, highest score 170. 45 wickets, ave. 27.55.

10. 2764 runs, ave. 46.06, highest score 187. 6 wickets, ave. 97.50.

22. W. G. Grace

There follow a few quizzes dedicated to some notable players of the past and present; it is fitting to begin with a sequence on the Doctor.

1. When might it have been said that Grace's future hung by a thread, or rather several threads?

2. In how many Tests did he play?

3. For which county side did he play after leaving Gloucestershire?

4. Whom did he kidnap, and why?

5. Grace is the only man to have scored 50,000 runs and taken 2000 wickets – true or false?

6. Why did he buy a new top-hat in 1895?

7. What was his best match bowling performance?

8. He took ten wickets in an innings and scored a century in the same match in 1886. Was this the first occasion on which the feat had been performed?

9. Grace scored 1000 runs in May, in fewer innings than anybody else has reached the same target – true or false?

10. At what sport, other than cricket, did he represent England?

23. J. B. Hobbs

If Grace was the Champion, Hobbs was rightly acclaimed as the Master, and the next quiz must therefore be about him.

1. For which minor county did Hobbs play?

2. With which two other Surrey players did he open for England?

3. When did he head the first-class bowling averages?

4. With whom did he most often score 100 or more for the first wicket, and how often did they achieve the feat?

5. In whose benefit match did he score his last century?

6. How many times did he score two centuries in a match?

7. What was the greatest number of centuries he scored in a season?

8. What was the significance of his score of 266 not out?

9. And of his 316 not out (apart from its being Hobbs' own highest score)?

10. How many stands of over 200 for the first wicket, in Tests, was he concerned in?

24. Don Bradman

Sir Donald Bradman was unquestionably the most interesting cricketer of all, on the purely factual level, and it would not do to leave him out of a quiz book of this kind. The answers to some of these questions will indicate his supremacy.

1. Who was the only bowler to get Bradman out for a duck twice in Tests?

2. When he toured the United States and Canada in 1932, against which former England captain did he play?

3. How many boundaries did he hit in his record innings of 452?

4. How many times did he score 100 or more before lunch?

5. How many double-centuries did he score?

6. How many times was he out in the nineties in Test cricket?

7. Who dismissed him most often in Tests?

8. What was the earliest date on which he reached 1000 runs in an English season, and what was unusual about his dismissals?

9. Why was he fined £50 in 1930?

10. Under how many captains did he play in Tests?

25. Walter Hammond

Hammond was a contemporary of Bradman's and, had the Don not taken to cricket (he was a fine lawn-tennis player and is said to have hesitated between the two games before settling for cricket), it is Hammond who would probably now be regarded as the greatest run-getter of all time.

1. Where was Hammond born?

2. What was his score in his first first-class innings?

3. Where did he make his first Test appearance?

4. What was his best bowling performance in a Test innings?

5. And in a first-class innings?

6. He holds the record for the greatest number of sixes hit in a Test innings. How many, and what was the occasion?

7. With whom did he put on 264 in a Test in 1939?

8. How many times did he head the English batting averages for the first-class season?

9. How many double-centuries did he score in Tests?

10. What was his highest score in county cricket?

26. Len Hutton

For the reader of my own generation, a few questions on one of the great men of our youth. Younger readers will no doubt do just as well.

1. How many Test centuries did Hutton score?

2. What was his highest score as England captain?

3. In which season did he score 3429 runs?

4. We all know what his highest first-class score was; but what was his second highest, and against whom did he make it?

5. On which ground did he score most first-class runs?

6. And on which ground did he score most Test runs?

7. Who was his first opening partner in a Test match?

8. And in a first-class match?

9. What was the highest opening partnership in which he took part?

10. And what was the highest in which he took part in the County Championship?

27. Garfield Sobers

A few questions about another of cricket's knights – Sir Garfield Sobers.

1. How old was Sobers when he first appeared in a Test?

2. In how many Tests did he play before making his first century, which happened to be the highest innings ever played in Tests?

3. How many runs did he score, in all, in that series?

4. His batting average for Nottinghamshire was lower than his average in Tests – true or false?

5. What was the highest partnership in which he shared?

6. How many catches did he make in Tests?

7. For which Australian state did he play?

8. What was his highest Test score in England?

9. He holds the record for the greatest number of catches taken by one fielder (other than a wicket-keeper) off one bowler in Tests. Who is the bowler?

10. Where did he score two hundreds in a Test?

28. Ian Botham

I include a chapter on the best-known England cricketer of our day, but it is rather difficult to devise questions that are sufficiently testing, so well-known are all his achievements.

1. In what county was Botham born?

2. He first came to the notice of the cricket public outside Somerset with a sensational performance in a one-day match against Hampshire. How many runs did he score?

3. What feat did he perform in his first Test; did he score fifty, take five wickets, or hold five catches?

4. Since then he has played for England in every Test, except when injured – true or false?

5. In which of his Tests did he reach the 'double' of 1000 runs and 100 wickets, and whose record did he beat?

6. He was the first player to score 100 runs and take ten wickets in the same Test – is this true or false?

7. What is his highest first-class score?

8. Against whom did he take his only hat-trick?

9. He finished off the fourth Test of the 1981 series with a remarkable bowling performance, taking the last five Australian wickets in – how many balls?

10. How many runs did he and Graham Dilley put on for the eighth wicket in the third Test of the same series?

29. The Chappells

The Chappell brothers have not, perhaps, been the best-loved characters to represent Australia, but they have performed some mighty deeds which I commemorate here.

1. What is the greatest number of catches taken in a Test series by any of the Chappells?

2. What Test catching record does one of them share with Yajuvendra Singh of India?

3. Which other player once described Ian Chappell as the best batsman in the world, at the start of a series in which he was to achieve very little?

4. How many times have Ian and Greg Chappell both scored hundreds in the same Test?

5. Which man has played under Greg Chappell in every Test in which he has captained Australia?

6. How many partnerships of over 200 have Ian and Greg shared in Tests?

7. What is Ian Chappell's highest Test score?

8. And what is Greg's best bowling performance in a Test innings?

9. Under how many captains has Ian played in Tests?

10. Greg has captained Australia more times than any other player – true or false?

30. Wicket-keepers

Wicket-keeping records attract rather less attention than those connected with batting or bowling, but they can be full of interest.

1. Which are the three leading combinations of wicket-keeper and bowler in Tests; that is, which keepers have caught or stumped most batsmen off one bowler?

2. Who was the first wicket-keeper to dismiss 1500 batsmen in first-class cricket?

3. And who was the first to dismiss 100 in Tests?

4. Which keeper dismissed 100 or more batsmen in three separate seasons?

5. Who conceded no byes in his first two innings against Australia, while over a thousand runs were scored?

6. Who is the only keeper to have made eight catches in a first-class innings?

7. Who stumped all three batsmen in a hat-trick?

8. Who stumped over 400 batsmen in the course of his first-class career?

9. Who scored 182 in an innings and held six catches in an innings, in the same Test?

10. Who was the first man to catch eleven batsmen in a first-class match?

31. True or false?

I have included some 'true or false' questions elsewhere in the book, but this miscellany may set a few problems.

1. A substitute, i.e. somebody not playing in the match, has made a stumping in a Test.

2. Nobody has ever made 100 catches in a season.

3. Nobody has been out 'hit the ball twice' in a Test.

4. G. F. Grace is the only man to have been dismissed for a 'pair' in his first Test for England.

5. No batsman has scored 1000 runs in a calendar month twice in the same season.

6. Tom Hayward was the first man to score 3000 runs in a season.

7. Two sides played Test cricket for England on the same day for the first time in 1929–30.

8. A bowler has taken all ten wickets in an innings without assistance from the fielders.

9. No bowler has taken all ten wickets and done the hat-trick in the same innings.

10. A batsman has scored eight double-centuries in his career, but never played in Test cricket.

32. Middlesex

I thought of including a quiz on each of the first-class counties but decided that this ran the risk of becoming tedious. I have made an arbitrary decision to include sections on each of the counties traditionally identified as the Big Six. I begin with Middlesex, tenants at cricket's headquarters.

1. Which Middlesex player captained Test teams of which his county captain was a member?

2. Who was the last Middlesex bowler to take 100 wickets in a season (in all matches)?

3. Who took most catches in a career (as a fielder, not a wicket-keeper) for Middlesex?

4. Who played the highest individual innings for Middlesex?

5. And who recorded the best bowling performance, in one innings?

6. Which future Prime Minister played for Middlesex?

7. Which Middlesex player twice reached his fifty in 12 scoring strokes?

8. And which scored 180 before lunch (though not for Middlesex)?

9. Who had a hand in opening partnerships of over 100 in both innings of a match in 1980, but with different partners?

10. Which Australian was capped for Middlesex after the second world war?

33. Surrey

Now we cross the river, to look at Middlesex's metropolitan rivals.

1. What is the highest innings total yet made for Surrey?

2. Who took most wickets for Surrey in first-class cricket?

3. What is Surrey's best result so far in the John Player League?

4. Which Surrey captain played hockey in the Olympic Games?

5. Who were the last Surrey pair to open the batting for England?

6. And who was the last Surrey wicket-keeper to keep for England?

7. For how many seasons did Stuart Surridge lead Surrey?

8. Which Surrey player has come nearest to scoring 100 centuries, without doing so?

9. Who was the Australian who played for Surrey before the first world war, scoring 4195 runs and taking 101 wickets?

10. What is Surrey's highest innings total since the second world war?

34. Yorkshire

Over the years, Yorkshire's record far outshines those of all other counties. Partly because they have stuck firmly to the policy of playing only native-born players, the county has had little success of late, yet Yorkshire are still the side everybody wants to beat.

1. Who was the first man to score centuries in his first Test against Australia, and in his last?

2. Which Yorkshireman hit ten sixes in an innings in 1932?

3. Which Yorkshireman toured Australia with a Test-playing MCC team but never played in a Test in his career?

4. And, similarly, who from Yorkshire toured the West Indies but never played in a Test?

5. Which Yorkshireman made his debut for England in his benefit year, at the age of 39?

6. Who played in every Championship match for Yorkshire for 14 consecutive seasons?

7. Which Yorkshire father and son played in Test cricket?

8. Which Yorkshire wicket-keeper dismissed more than 1300 batsmen but never played in a Test?

9. Who scored a century for Yorkshire on his debut in 1981?

10. Who took all ten wickets for 35 for Yorkshire in 1914?

35. Lancashire

Like Yorkshire, Lancashire have fallen on comparatively
hard times lately (except in the Gillette Cup) but the county
has a glorious history. I have tried to provide a balance of
ancient and modern questions.

1. Which Test star was recalled to the England colours in
    1956, with startling success?

2. When did Lancashire win a Championship match
    without losing a wicket?

3. Which Lancashire opening batsman once carried his
    bat for 5?

4. Who made a sensational match-winning catch for
    Lancashire in a Gillette Cup final?

5. Who was the last Lancashire player to score a double-
    century for England?

6. Who ended his Test career when he published a
    criticism of his captain's management of the bowling?

7. Which two Australians made a record ninth-wicket
    stand for Lancashire?

8. Who once scored 34 runs off a six-ball over for
    Lancashire?

9. Who, since the second world war, played for England
    in the season of his first-class debut for Lancashire?

10. Name two Lancashire bowlers who played for England
    in the Victory Tests of 1945 but never played in official
    Tests.

36. Kent

Kent are in some ways the most glamorous of county teams; they play on some attractive grounds and have some remarkable feats of scoring to their credit. They have also had some remarkable players, a few of whom are celebrated here.

1. Who made a century on his debut for Kent while still at school?

2. Who captained Kent in 1970, when they won the Championship for the first time for 57 years?

3. How many times have Kent reached the final of a major one-day competition?

4. Who has taken most catches in a season for Kent (as a fielder)?

5. Against whom did Kent make their highest-ever score, and where?

6. Which bowler took more wickets in a season for Kent than all his team-mates put together?

7. Who was 'Punter'?

8. Which three Kent brothers played in Tests?

9. Which Kent wicket-keeper conceded 48 byes and 23 leg-byes in an innings?

10. Which former Kent player, when acting as a Test umpire, declined to take the field as a protest against the conduct of one of the teams?

37. Nottinghamshire

Modern followers of the game may raise an eyebrow at the inclusion of Notts among the Big Six but, until they fell on hard times in the post-war era, they were consistently near the head of the table. Even today, they have won more games than they have lost against each other county outside the Big Six – as good a definition of worthiness as any other.

1. Which three Notts bowlers took most Championship wickets in 1981?

2. Who made the highest-ever score for Notts, and where did he do so?

3. Which Notts leg-spinner played just once for England?

4. What is S. H. Copley's claim to fame?

5. Who was the last Notts man to captain England?

6. Who had a gap of 18 years between his eleventh and twelfth Tests?

7. Who scored 98 in a Test when batting as a night-watchman?

8. The best bowling performances for and against Notts are both 17 for 89 – who were the two bowlers?

9. Which Notts man played for England in 1947, making his Test debut at the age of 34, and what was his nick-name?

10. Who scored over 2000 runs for Notts in each of his last four seasons, dying before he could appear again?

38. Some great Test players

All the questions in this sequence relate to players who have achieved great things in Tests.

The first five players to be named have all scored over 5000 Test runs.

1. Who was the second Australian to do so?

2. Which English batsman holds the record for the greatest number of runs scored against one other country?

3. And which Englishman has scored over 1000 runs against each of four other countries?

4. Who has scored the fastest 300 in a Test?

5. And who has scored most Test runs on a single ground?

The next five questions all relate to bowlers who have taken over 200 Test wickets.

6. Who conceded most runs in a Test series?

7. Of the bowlers who took over 200 wickets, who has the worst bowling average?

8. Who was nicknamed 'The Whippet'?

9. Who took the record number of wickets in a South African first-class season?

10. Whose best first-class performance was the taking of seven wickets for five runs?

39. Some great Test matches

The aim here is to recall ten great Tests, giving a clue or two to each. Which are the matches referred to?

1. A batsman scored 100 in 75 minutes in the fourth innings?

2. For the first time in a Test, a side scored over 400 in the fourth innings and won.

3. For the first time, a side scored over 700 in a Test innings in England.

4. A bowler took seven wickets in an innings and opened the batting, both on the first day of a Test.

5. A batsman scored over 200 in a crisis, and was not picked again for over seven years.

6. Two 20-year-olds bowled over 100 overs in a day.

7. England's opening pair scored 172 for the first wicket on a difficult pitch, and England won the match.

8. The crowd helped to drain the wicket, and England won the match in the last ten minutes.

9. Australia were bowled out for 111, losing their last eight wickets for 36.

10. Set 438 to win, a side made 429 for 8, their opening batsman setting a new record for his team.

40.   Cricket books

Cricket, more than any other game, is rich in its literature. Many fascinating books have been written about it by men of letters, journalists and some highly intelligent players. I present here clues to the subject-matter of ten books – of varying merit, it must be admitted.

1.   Written by a notable fast bowler, who was honest enough to admit in it that he tried to score hits on the batsmen – though of course with no serious intention of maiming them!
2.   Autobiography of an England captain, born in the West Indies, who played cricket in almost every country under the sun.
3.   Biography of a famous fast bowler and cricket personality, which is generally reckoned the best work of a brilliant and prolific writer.
4.   A book of photographs of a single series, taken by the leading cricket photographer of the day, the narrative written by one who was concerned in his first tour book for eighteen years.
5.   Biographies of all Australia's Test captains.
6.   Punning title of an account of a controversial series. The pun may have been thrown away on readers who knew nothing of polo!
7.   A description of a Test series written by a critic who was not present at the matches and admitted as much in the title.
8.   An account of some aspects of West Indian cricket, and much else besides, written by a distinguished West Indian writer who was a close friend of Lord Constantine.
9.   A collection of essays, including a critique of the most famous cricket poem of all, and some thoughts on a player who had a spectacularly brief first-class career.
10.   A highly romantic cricket story, allegedly written by a leading England batsman.

ANSWERS

1. The 1982 season

1. M. W. Gatting of Middlesex completed his 1000 runs on 26 June. This was late by pre-war standards (the latest this century has been Richard Lumb on 13 July 1979); the second man in 1982 was Alvin Kallicharran, who got there on 9 July.

2. D. E. East of Essex, playing in his first full season.

3. Ian Botham, in the second Test against India, the fiftieth of his career.

4. Worcestershire played Kent at Hereford.

5. Khitar Hayat.

6. Jalal-ud-Din, who was called up when Sarfraz Nawaz and Imran Khan were injured early in the tour. He played in several matches but was injured himself when the team was picked for the final Test, whereupon Ehtesham-ud-Din was called up from Daisy Hill, in the Bolton League.

7. N. E. Briers, who scored 91 not out and 93 not out against Somerset. Leicestershire were making a spirited run in the Championship at the time, and Roger Tolchard had to sacrifice Briers in a good cause. Leicestershire won the match and finished second in the Championship; Tolchard and Briers are to be congratulated on putting the game before the individual.

8. P. R. Downton, in a bizarre mix-up at Southend. Downton, who had been injured, was batting with K. P. Tomlins as his runner. He played the ball and forgot that Tomlins was assisting. Both made good their ground at the bowler's end, but Essex knew the Laws (Laws 2.7 and 38 in this case) and broke the wicket at the striker's end. Downton was correctly given out.

9. J. F. Steele of Leicestershire, who took 52 wickets at 20.67 apiece – a commentary on the state of English cricket, perhaps, since Steele would hardly claim to be a major bowler.

10. A. Needham of Surrey, who scored 134 not out against Lancashire, putting on 172 for the tenth wicket with R. Jackman. Next day he took 5 for 91, and concluded a memorable match by incurring his committee's displeasure for celebrating not wisely but too well. A real old-fashioned county pro!

2. England v. Australia, 1877-1938

1. At Trent Bridge in 1938, L. Hutton scored 100, C. J. Barnett 126, E. Paynter 216 not out and D. C. S. Compton 102 when England scored 658 for 8 declared. Barnett scored 98 before lunch, and he and Hutton put on 219 for the first wicket. Hutton and Compton were playing in their first Test against Australia. In Australia's first innings, S. J. McCabe scored 232 not out, making 72 out of 77 for the last wicket. Australia were out for 411 and followed on; in the second innings W. A. Brown scored 133 and D. G. Bradman 144 not out. Bradman batted for 365 minutes; it was his slowest Test century.

2. At Sydney, in January 1887. A. Shrewsbury, W. Barnes, W. Gunn, W. H. Scotton, W. Flowers and M. Sherwin, all Nottinghamshire players, appeared in the England side which won by 13 runs.

3. In the first Test, Australia were represented by players who had been on the previous summer's tour of England, but they demanded 50 per cent of the gate money for the second match, which the ground authority refused to pay. The Australian team for the second Test contained nine new caps and lost by ten wickets.

4. Tom Richardson took 10 for 156 in the third Test of 1893, and Ken Farnes 10 for 179 in the first of 1934.

5. Herbert Sutcliffe, at Melbourne. He made 176 and 127 in the second Test of the 1924–25 series, and 143 in the fourth. He followed this by making 58 and 135 in the third Test of 1928–29. It was perhaps fortunate for the Australians that he was unfit to play in the fifth Test of the 1928–29 series, the only one they won.

6. 1905. F. S. Jackson and J. Darling were both born on 21 November 1870.

7. D. G. Bradman's 270 at Adelaide in 1937. It was over-taken by R. B. Simpson's 311 at Manchester in 1964.

8. This is true. England beat Australia by an innings and 21 runs at Manchester in 1888, the match ending at 1.55 on the second day. The scores were: England 172, Australia 81 (Peel 7 for 31) and 70 (Peel 4 for 37). 200.2 four-ball overs were bowled.

9. Clem Hill, who scored 2660 against England. Hobbs overtook him in 1926.

10. In 1912. It was agreed to play the final match of the first and only Triangular Tournament to a finish if the result of the Tournament depended on it. Before the match England had won three games and Australia two, and the match was therefore played out, England winning in four days by 244 runs.

3. England v. Australia, 1946-81

1. Len Hutton put Australia in at Brisbane in 1954, and his side lost by an innings and 154 runs. Scores: Australia 601 for 8 dec. (Morris 153, Harvey 162), England 190 and 257. However, England won the series 3-1.

2. Peter May scored 113 at Melbourne in 1958-59; he was the first England captain to do so in Australia since A. C. MacLaren scored 116 in 1901.

3. P. H. Edmonds, in 1975.

4. Lindwall went down with chickenpox during the first Test of the 1946-47 series, and F. W. Freer replaced him for the second match at Sydney. He took 1 for 25 and 2 for 49, and scored 28 not out, but was not picked again.

5. R. M. Cowper. When he went in in the fifth Test of the 1965-66 series, played at Melbourne, Australia were 36 for 2 in reply to England's 485 for 9 declared. Cowper scored 307 in 727 minutes, which is not only the longest first-class innings played in Australia but the fifth longest played anywhere. The record is held by Hanif Mohammad (970 minutes), followed by L. Hutton (797 minutes), R. B. Simpson (762 minutes) and Rashid Israr (750 minutes).

6. K. F. Barrington scored 104, 52, 52 not out, 63, 132 not out in 1962-63 and 69, 51, 63, 60, and 102 in 1965-66.

7. The second Test at Lord's in 1956. G. R. A. Langley caught eight and stumped one; T. G. Evans caught six and stumped one.

8. In 1950, at Brisbane. Australia had scored 228 on the first day, and when England batted on the third day, the second having been washed out, they lost seven wickets for 68 before F. R. Brown declared. Australia

then made 32 for 7, declared, and England lost a further six wickets for 30 before the close. On the following day, England were all out for 122 and lost the match by 70 runs.

9. G. Boycott, in the third Test of the 1977 series (he scored 107 and 80 not out), and K. J. Hughes in the Centenary Test of 1980 (he scored 117 and 84). M. L. Jaisimha also batted on all five days when India drew with Australia at Calcutta in 1960.

10. The fifth Test at the Oval in 1972, which lasted for 1937 minutes.

4. England v. South Africa

1. Walter Lees of Surrey took 26 wickets at an average of 17.96 in the series of 1905–06, which South Africa won 4–1. England were not represented by a strong team and, although Lees did extraordinarily well, he was replaced by the 'first-team' players in the next home series.

2. H. D. ('Hopper') Read of Essex, a genuinely fast bowler who was having a good season, played at the Oval in 1935. He took 4 for 136 and 2 for 64, dismissing Mitchell (twice), Viljoen, Cameron, Dalton and Nourse. However, he was prevented by the claims of business from playing in subsequent seasons; this is not one of those omissions for which one can blame the selectors.

3. W. L. Murdoch, A. E. Trott, S. M. J. Woods and J. J. Ferris.

4. S. F. Barnes had the remarkable figures of 83 wickets for 818, an average of 9.86, in seven Tests in 1912 and 1913–14. In the latter series he took 49 wickets in four matches, which remains the record for a single series.

5. Arthur Mitchell was so summoned to play in the third Test at Leeds in 1935, when M. Leyland was injured. He scored 58 and 72.

6. J. P. Duminy, who had previously played in two Tests at home without success, was called up by the 1929 tourists and played at Leeds, scoring 2 and 12.

7. H. G. Owen-Smith, in that same game at Leeds in 1929. He came in at 73 for 5 in the second innings, with South Africa still 19 behind, and made 129. He and Bell scored 103 in 65 minutes for the last wicket, which remains the South African Test record. He was aged 20 years 148 days at the time.

8. Thirteen. They are Lord's (London), the Oval, Old Trafford, Trent Bridge, Headingley, Edgbaston, Port Elizabeth, Cape Town, Lord's (Durban), Kingsmead (Durban), Old Wanderers (Johannesburg), Ellis Park (Johannesburg) and New Wanderers (Johannesburg).

9. Hugh Tayfield took 4 for 79 and 9 for 113 (13 for 192 in the match) against England at Johannesburg in 1957.

10. This is true. In 1905–06, South Africa's team in all five Tests was: P. W. Sherwell (captain), L. J. Tancred, W. A. Shalders, G. C. White, A. W. Nourse, C. M. H. Hathorn, G. A. Faulkner, J. H. Sinclair, S. J. Snooke, R. O. Schwarz and A. E. E. Vogler.

5. England v. West Indies

1. J. B. Stollmeyer scored 59 and his brother, V. H. Stoll-
    meyer, 96 in the third Test at the Oval in 1939 (V. H.'s
    only Test). G. C. and R. S. Grant are the only other pair of
    brothers to have played for the West Indies against
    England.

2. At Old Trafford in 1976, England made 71, including 19
    extras, and 126, including 25 extras. The highest-scoring
    batsman was D. S. Steele with 20 and 15. This is the only
    occasion in Test cricket that extras have 'outscored' all
    the batsmen on a side in a match, although it has
    happened several times in a single innings.

3. 1969, when England won 2–0, with one match drawn.

4. At Kingston in 1930, England made 849 and 272 for 9
    declared, totalling 1121. 1000 has only been exceeded
    on three other occasions in Test cricket: at the Oval in
    1934, Australia made 701 and 327; at Durban in 1939,
    South Africa made 530 and 481; and at Sydney in 1969,
    Australia made 619 and 394 for 9 declared.

5. At the Oval in 1966, England's score went from 166 for 7
    to 527 all out. T. W. Graveney (165) and J. T. Murray (112)
    added 217 for the eighth wicket, and K. Higgs (63) and
    J. A. Snow (59 not out) added 128 for the tenth wicket.

6. At Lord's in 1973, R. B. Kanhai made 157, G. S. Sobers
    150 and B. D. Julien 121, in the West Indies score of 652
    for 8 declared.

7. In 1976, when West Indies, playing at Leeds, made 147
    for 0 by lunch, 330 for 2 by tea, and 437 for 9 by the close
    on the first day. They were all out for 450. England made
    387 and the West Indies were all out for 196 in the
    second innings. Set to get 260 to win, England were at
    one stage 140 for 4, but were all out for 204, losing by 55.

8. K. H. Weekes, at the Oval in 1939.

9. At Lord's in 1966, the West Indies were headed by 86 on the first innings, and they were 95 for 5 in the second when G. S. Sobers was joined by his cousin D. A. J. Holford. They added 274 without being parted which is still the West Indies sixth-wicket record.

10. At Port-of-Spain in 1968, West Indies led England by 122 on the first innings, and Sobers declared at 92 for 2 in the second, setting England to make 215 in 165 minutes. They won with three minutes to spare.

6. English Test cricketers

1. The Hon. C. J. Coventry and B. A. F. Grieve made their first first-class appearances (for England) in the first Test ever played between England and South Africa, in South Africa in 1889. J. E. P. McMaster made his first-class debut, also for England, in the second Test a fortnight later. The touring side was clearly an unrepresentative one and the games, other than the Tests, were played against odds and were not first-class. This is believed to have been McMaster's only first-class appearance.

2. Geoffrey Boycott went in at no. 4 in each innings of the third Test at Bridgetown in 1974, but otherwise always opened. Sir Jack Hobbs went in down the order five times, and Sir Leonard Hutton on seven occasions. Only once did Herbert Sutcliffe not open the innings, but he does not qualify as he did not bat 100 times in Tests (his figure is 84 innings).

3. Sir Jack Hobbs made 211 at Lord's against South Africa in 1924.

4. J. H. Edrich hit five sixes and 52 fours – 238 in all – when he scored 310 not out against New Zealand at Leeds in 1965.

5. J. T. Tyldesley, in 1904. This is the highest percentage of a completed Test innings score to be made by an Englishman, although D. L. Amiss did slightly better when he made 262 not out out of 432–9 at Kingston in 1974. Tyldesley's percentage was 60.1, Amiss's 60.6.

6. L. E. G. Ames scored 123 before lunch on the third day against South Africa at the Oval in 1935.

7. G. F. Grace, who died of a chill only a fortnight after playing in his only Test, in 1880. He made a 'pair of spectacles', but also brought off one of the most famous catches in Test history. George Bonnor made an immense hit – it is said to have travelled 115 yards, though this is a little hard to believe. The ball certainly went very high, and the batsmen were on their third run before it came down into Fred Grace's safe hands.

8. James Southerton, who played in the first two Tests ever played. He is the oldest player ever to make a first Test appearance, having been 49 years 119 days old on the first day of the first Test. He was a slow off-spinner who represented Surrey, Sussex and Hampshire; in those more relaxed days, he played for all three in the same season.

9. J. C. W. MacBryan suffered this unique misfortune. He was picked against South Africa in a rather experimental team in 1924, but the match, at Manchester, was ruined by rain. Some leading players were recalled for the next Test, and MacBryan never got another chance.

10. L. Hutton, C. Washbrook, D. C. S. Compton, W. R. Hammond, J. Hardstaff jr, P. A. Gibb, D. V. P. Wright, W. E. Bowes, W. Voce, L. B. Fishlock, W. J. Edrich, James Langridge, N. W. D. Yardley, W. E. Hollies, C. J. Barnett, W. H. Copson, G. O. B. Allen, F. R. Brown, A. R. Gover.

7. Australian Test cricketers

1. G. Coulthard, who in 1881 umpired in the third Test ever played and took part in the sixth; he batted at no. 11 and did not bowl. He was the first, not the only, because P. G. McShane umpired in the fourth, and played in the fifth, Tests of 1884 – 85.

2. George Giffen, bowling for an Australian XI against a Combined XI of Australia; this was one of a series of matches played by the 1884 touring team before they sailed for England.

3. Dr Roland Pope, who accompanied several touring teams in England as honorary medical adviser, guide, philosopher and friend. He played in eight first-class matches in all, on the tours of 1886, 1890 and 1902.

4. G. S. Chappell has caught 21 batsmen (to date) off the bowling of D. K. Lillee and R. N. Harvey caught 21 off R. Benaud.

5. George Giffen. The tour was that of 1893 and George, who had done the double in 1886, did so again. He had been unavailable in 1888 and 1890, the intervening tours. His brother, Walter, was somewhat less successful, scoring 170 runs at an average of 12.14. Even this average was boosted by a score of 62 against Oxford and Cambridge Universities Past and Present. As Walter Giffen came in to bat at 701 for 8, the best that can be said of his innings is that he took the opportunity that was offered him.

6. S. E. Gregory, nicknamed 'Little Tich'. He was a member of every touring team between 1890 and 1912, captaining the last-named in the disastrous Triangular Tournament of that year. Australia had a very weak team because several leading players had quarrelled with the Board of Control and refused to tour, and the season was a very wet one. Gregory himself batted manfully and never lost heart, but the team had rather too many passengers.

7. Hugh Trumble, who dismissed Bosanquet, Warner and Lilley in the fifth Test of the 1903–04 series.

8. B. N. Jarman, who took over from the injured W. M. Lawry for the fourth Test of the 1968 series. The match is something of a curiosity, in that M. C. Cowdrey, the appointed England captain, was also injured and T. W. Graveney led the side. (R. W. Marsh has taken over the leadership of the Australian side on the field on more than one occasion, but has never been appointed captain for a Test.)

9. In 1958–59, English critics found the actions of I. Meckiff, G. F. Rorke and J. W. Burke more than suspect; some also expressed doubts about K. N. Slater, who played his only Test in that series. Meckiff was subsequently no-balled in the first Test of 1963–64, and announced his retirement.

10. G. D McKenzie, at Lord's in 1961. R. Benaud was injured, and R. N. Harvey led Australia for the only time. They won by five wickets, England's first defeat at home for five years. This was the start of a highly successful Test career in which McKenzie took 246 wickets.

8. South African Test cricketers

1. A. Melville scored 189 and 104 not out in the first Test against England in 1947, and B. Mitchell scored 120 and 189 not out in the fifth Test in the same year. They are, in fact, the only two South Africans to score a century in each innings in any Test.

2. R. G. Pollock, who made 122 and 175 against Australia, and 137 against England.

3. Xenophon Balaskas, the only cricketer of Greek descent to swing a Test match, who took 5 for 49 and 4 for 54 in South Africa's first Test win in England, at Lord's in 1935. (A. J. Traicos, also of Greek descent, played in South Africa's last three Test matches in 1970.)

4. Clive Van Ryneveld, who played in 19 Tests between 1951 and 1958 and played in four rugby Internationals for England while at Oxford University. M. K. Elgie later played cricket for South Africa and rugby for Scotland.

5. H. M. Taberer captained South Africa against the 1902 Australians. His side did well up to a point, forcing Australia to follow on, but the tourists made 372 for 7 declared in the second innings (in which Taberer bowled Trumper for 37) and saved the game with some ease. Nevertheless, Taberer can be counted as a little unlucky to have been dropped. In the next Test, J. H. Anderson, also playing in his only Test, took over the captaincy and Australia won.

6. E. J. Barlow and R. G. Pollock made 341 for the third wicket in the fourth Test against Australia in 1964. Barlow scored 201 and Pollock 175, and South Africa won by ten wickets.

7. R. O. Schwarz, A. E. E. Vogler, G. C. White and G. A. Faulkner. The googly was then a relatively new weapon, and South Africa had had a comfortable win in South Africa in 1905–06. The bowlers did well in 1907, but it was a very wet summer and the South African

batsmen made little of the conditions. England won the only Test of the three to be finished, Colin Blythe getting the better of all the South African batsmen and finishing with 15 for 99.

8. G. A. Faulkner scored 732 against Australia in 1910–11.

9. A. Melville, in 1938–39 and 1947.

10. This was G. A. Faulkner again; his brilliance as an all-rounder is sometimes overlooked by modern students of the game. In 1912 he scored 1075 runs at an average of 23.88, and took 163 wickets at 15.42 apiece.

9. West Indian Test cricketers

1. The Test teams were at that time selected by the local associations and not by the Board of Control. Not surprisingly, each association picked one of its own men as captain; they were E. L. G. Hoad (Barbados), N. Betancourt (Trinidad), M. P. Fernandes (British Guiana, as Guyana was then called), and R. K. Nunes (Jamaica). Altogether, 28 players represented West Indies in the four Tests and in the circumstances, they did well to halve the series 1–1.

2. This happened in 1978. The Australians had a very inexperienced side because many of their players had joined World Series Cricket, while the WSC players in the West Indies squad played in the first two Tests but refused to accept selection for the third because some of their number had been omitted as being unable to commit themselves to a forthcoming tour. The successful batsmen were H. A. Gomes and A. B. Williams (West Indies), and G. M. Wood and C. S. Serjeant (Australia).

3. D. S. Atkinson made 219 at Bridgetown in 1955 and took part in a stand of 347 with C. C. Depeiza, which remains the world seventh-wicket record for all first-class cricket.

4. This is true. The record is 98 (unbroken) set by F. M. M. Worrell and W. W. Hall against India in 1962.

5. Hammond A. Furlonge, Simpson C. Guillen, and George McDonald Carew.

6. Wesley Hall took 4 for 140 and 5 for 63. The other West Indian bowlers took only six wickets between them, five Australians being run out.

7. C. A. Roach scored 122 in the first innings of the first Test of the 1929–30 series, the fourth Test played by the West Indies. G. A. Headley scored 176 in the second innings of the same test.

Picture Quiz

(Answers on page 128)

1. Who is the batsman, and for which wicket does he hold the Test partnership record?

2. What match is pictured here, and who are the players?

Sport & General

Central Press

Central Pres

3. The batsman batted in every position from no. 3 to no.11 in Tests. The catcher held 1.96 catches per Test. Their names?

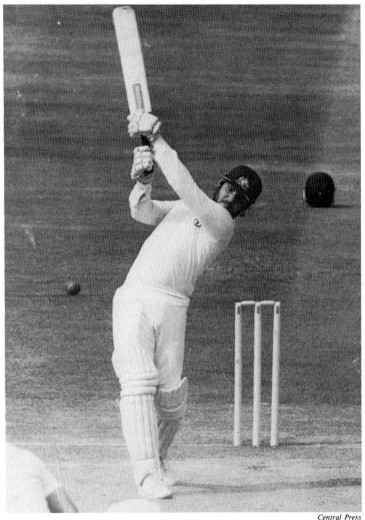

4. A discarded fielding helmet is placed on the ground. What runs accrue to the batting side if it is struck by the ball, and has this happened in a Test?

Central Press

5. What is the occasion, and who are the two characters at the centre of the stage?

6. This man played in five Tests on one tour and in four Tests at home, each in a different season. Who is he?

Central Press

7. Who is this batsman, and when did he go in first for England?

8. He scored more runs after his last Test than did any other player. Who is he, and approximately how many did he score?

Central Press

9. He set a unique record in 1982. Who is he, and what was
the record?

10. How many Tests did England play between this man's forty-ninth Test and his fiftieth? And who is the wicket-keeper?

9. West Indian Test cricketers *(continued)*

8. E. S. M. Kentish. It is said that he went up to Oxford with the sole intention of getting a Blue (he was on a one-year course). Oxford had rather the worst of a draw, and it is difficult to feel very sorry for them.

9. C. G. Greenidge scored 134 and 101 in the third Test at Old Trafford, and 115 in the fourth Test at Leeds. He was the first man to score three hundreds in succession against England since A. R. Morris did so in 1947.

10. In 1971–72, against New Zealand.

10. New Zealand Test cricketers

1. G. M. Turner scored 141 not out, in a total of 169 for Worcestershire against Glamorgan at Swansea in 1977. This represented 83.4% of the total. The next highest percentage is 79.8; V. S. Hazare scored 309 out of a total of 387 for the Rest against Hindus at Bombay in 1943–44. The second highest percentage in England is 79.2: W. G. Grace's 126 out of 159 for the United South of England XI against the United North of England at Hull in 1876.

2. Horace Dennis Smith bowled Eddie Paynter with his first ball in Test cricket at Christchurch in 1933. Nevertheless, England went on to make 560 for 8 declared (Hammond 227, Ames 103) and Smith's figures were 20–0–113–1. He was not picked again.

3. J. A. Cowie, who took 114 wickets at 19.95 apiece on the 1937 tour of England, including 19 at 20.78 each in the three Tests.

4. Narotam Puna, who played in three Tests against England in 1965–66, without much success. His first-class record was more distinguished; he took 229 wickets at an average of 24.43, rather better figures than a number of New Zealand spinners of his period. He may have been a little unlucky not to have been capped more often.

5. P. J. Petherick, who dismissed Javed Miandad, Wasim Raja and Intikhab Alam with successive balls in his first Test at Lahore in 1976. He was only the second bowler to do the hat-trick in his first Test, M. J. C. Allom having done so for England against New Zealand in 1930. Statistically speaking, Petherick's was perhaps the second most distinguished 'bag' of all hat-tricks in Tests, in that all three of his victims went on to score over 1000 runs in Tests. J. T. Hearne dismissed C. Hill, S. E. Gregory and M. A. Noble in three balls at Leeds in 1899, and they were no doubt a more prestigious trio.

6. This dream-like debut was by B. R. Taylor at Calcutta in 1965. He scored 105 and 0 not out, and took 5 for 86 in the only innings in which he bowled.

7. A. M. Moir bowled the last over before tea and the first afterwards on the fourth day of the second Test against England in 1951. His action appears to have been inadvertent; on the only other occasion when a bowler bowled two consecutive overs in a Test (Warwick Armstrong doing so in the fourth Test of 1921) there is at least a possibility that the bowler did so deliberately. He had just put the England captain right on a point of law, and it may have appealed to his sense of humour to break a law in return.

8. D. A. R. Moloney, who played in three Tests in 1937 and died of wounds at El Alamein in 1942.

9. R. C. Motz, who had a remarkable success rate against Boycott. He bowled to him in twelve innings and dismissed him six times, twice for a duck.

10. H. G. Vivian, who made his debut against England in 1931 at the age of 18, and G. E. Vivian, who was 19 years and six days old when he first appeared against India in 1965. This was actually his first-class debut, and he is the last man to have made his first first-class appearance in a Test.

11. Indian Test cricketers

1. S. M. Gavaskar, who in the first three Tests of the 1977–78 series in Australia scored 3 and 113, 4 and 127, 0 and 118.

2. S. A. Durani, who scored 61 not out in 34 minutes against England at Kanpur in 1964, reaching his fifty in 29 minutes. It is fair to say that the game was completely dead at the time. England had scored 559 for 8 declared and dismissed India for 266, and India were 270 for 3 in their second innings when Durani came in. His runs were made off the bowling of Cowdrey and Parks, who had kept wicket until the closing stages. The only faster fifty, in terms of time, to be scored in a Test is credited to J. T. Brown, who reached his fifty in 28 minutes at Melbourne in 1895. The circumstances were somewhat different, in that he had gone in at 28 for 2 with England still needing 268 to win; he scored 140 and England won by six wickets.

3. P. Roy, who captained India at Lord's in 1959. His son made his Test debut in the 1981–82 series.

4. M. L. Jaisimha, playing against Pakistan at Kanpur in 1960. If he had completed his hundred, it would have been comfortably (if that is the right word) the slowest ever for India, but two men, Mudassar Nazar and D. J. McGlew, have taken longer to reach the hundred. The match at Kanpur was one of the dreariest ever played, the average run-rate being 155 per day, and only 23 wickets falling in five days.

5. P. R. Umrigar, who scored 223 in the first Test against New Zealand in 1955. M. H. ('Vinoo') Mankad then equalled his score in the second Test, and surpassed it with 231 in the fifth.

6. B. S. Chandrasekhar, arguably the worst batsman to play in Tests in modern times. He made 22 ducks in all, and scored 167 runs in 80 innings. It must have created a sensation when he and B. S. Bedi, another non-batsman, added 42 for the last wicket against New Zealand at Bombay in 1976.

7. P. Roy, the elder, who had a very bad time against England in 1952. He scored 19, 35, and those five ducks, of which Trueman was responsible for four and Bedser for one.

8. B. S. Bedi. A slow left-arm bowler, he took 266 wickets at 28.71 apiece, taking five wickets in an innings 14 times.

9. In the fifth Test of the 1955–56 series against New Zealand referred to in the answer to question 5, M. H. Mankad (231) and P. Roy (173) scored 413 for the first wicket. It is the Indian record for any wicket, and the world Test record for the first wicket; curiously, perhaps, it is only the ninth-best stand for the first wicket in first-class cricket.

10. V. L. Mehra, who was aged 17 years and 265 days when he played his first Test in the 1955–56 series against New Zealand which has already featured in the answers to questions 5 and 9. (It should be said that the dates of birth of Indian and Pakistani cricketers have to be taken on trust to some extent, the law on the registration of births being less stringent than in other countries.)

12. Pakistani Test cricketers

1. Miran Bux played in two Tests against India in 1955, at the age of 47. He scored one run in three innings (twice not out) and took two wickets for 115.

2. A. H. Kardar (also known as Abdul Hafeez), Amir Elahi and Gul Mahomed, all of whom played for both India and Pakistan.

3. Mushtaq Mohammad and Asif Iqbal put on 350 for the fourth wicket against New Zealand in 1973, taking the score from 126 to 476. Mushtaq scored 201 and Asif 175. Pakistan declared at 507 for 6 and won by an innings.

4. In the same Test, Mushtaq took 5 for 49 in the New Zealand second innings. He was the second player to score a double-century and take five wickets in an innings in the same Test, D. S. Atkinson having done so for the West Indies against Australia in 1955. Nobody has achieved the feat since.

5. In the second Test ever played by Pakistan, at Lucknow in 1952, Nazar Mohammad carried his bat against India for 124, made out of a total of 331 in 8 hours 35 minutes. Pakistan won by an innings and Nazar was the first man to be on the field throughout a completed Test match. At Lahore in 1977, his son, Mudassar Nazar, scored 114 against England. His century took him 9 hours 17 minutes, the slowest in all first-class cricket, and he batted for 9 hours 35 minutes in all. Pakistan declared at 407 for 8, but England saved the game with some ease.

6. Pakistan beat Australia in the first Test ever contested by the two countries, at Karachi in 1956. A. H. Kardar was the captain, as he had been when Pakistan first beat England in 1954. Apart from the unexpected result, the match was far from exciting. On the first day, Australia were put out for 80, compiled in 53.1 overs, and the whole day produced only 95 runs, the record 'low' for a full day's play in a Test. Pakistan made 199; Wazir Mohammad and Kardar himself scored 67 and 69 respectively, but nobody else reached 20. Australia were all out in the

second innings for 187 (Benaud 56) and Pakistan took 48.4 overs to score the 69 they needed to win. The whole match thus produced 535 runs in 304 overs. Fazal Mahmood took 13 wickets for 114 runs, still the Pakistani record.

7. Majid Khan, batting against New Zealand at Karachi in 1976. He made 108 before lunch but was out for 112. Pakistan scored 565 for 9 declared, Javed Miandad, at the age of 19, scoring 206 and Mushtaq Mohammad 107. New Zealand lost 5 wickets for 104 and 6 for 195, but recovered to make 468 thanks to a seventh-wicket stand of 186 between Lees (152) and Richard Hadlee (87). Pakistan made 290 for 5 declared in their second innings, Majid being run out for 50, and New Zealand, scoring 262 for 7, saved the game.

8. Taslim Arif, in a rather remarkable match against Australia at Faisalabad in 1980. After the first day had been washed out, Australia scored 617 (G. Chappell 235, Yallop 172) and Pakistan had nothing but a draw to play for. They batted in lively fashion against some rather relaxed bowling (all eleven Australians bowled) and Taslim made his 210 not out in $7\frac{1}{4}$ hours.

9. Fazal Mahmood took 20 of the 43 England wickets to fall in the 1954 series. He was mastered in the second Test at Nottingham, where he took 0 for 148, but had a full revenge at the Oval, taking 12 for 99 and bowling his side to their first win against England.

10. Zaheer Abbas scored 274 in 1971, the highest by any batsman in his first innings against England, and 240 in 1974. Pakistan made 608 for 7 declared on the first occasion and 600 for 7 declared on the second, but England saved both matches.

13.   Australia v. West Indies

1.   Norman O'Neill scored 181 for Australia. Garfield Sobers made 132 for the West Indies, and there were no fewer than ten fifties, credited to nine different players; only Frank Worrell made two.

2.   I. R. Redpath was 'done' by C. C. Griffith in the fourth Test of 1968–69. Although Griffith was very much criticised, it is fair to say that Australia were bustling for runs at the time, and had been taking some very short ones. It is quite probable that Redpath had been stealing a yard or two, and I personally cannot see that the convention which says that the bowler should always warn the backer-up before running him out is a fair or sensible one. Most cricketing conventions are observed for the protection of the batsman and, in a Test, he should be able to live without them.

3.   M. A. Holding took 11 for 107 at Melbourne in December 1981, overtaking the 10 for 113 taken by G. E. Gomez at Sydney in 1952. Holding also holds the record for West Indies against England, having taken 14 for 149 at the Oval in 1976.

4.   Miller (137) and Lindwall (118) at Bridgetown. Australia scored 668, and the match was drawn.

5.   At Adelaide in December 1930, G. C. Grant scored 53 not out and 71 not out, but Australia won by ten wickets.

6.   This happened in Georgetown in 1965, when the local Umpires' Association told one of its members not to stand because they disagreed with the choice of the other umpire, a Barbadian. The West Indies Board asked G. E. Gomez, one of the selectors, who held an umpire's certificate but had never stood in a first-class match, to officiate, and he did so with distinction. He also summarised the play on the radio each evening; whether he poured the tea as well is not on the record.

7.   Fredericks reached his hundred in 71 balls in the course of his 169 at Perth in 1975. Modern over-rates being what they are, his century took him 116 minutes.

G. L. Jessop's hundred at the Oval in 1902 took 75 balls, and 75 minutes. The only Test century for any country which may have taken fewer balls than that of Fredericks was J. M. Gregory's at Johannesburg in 1921. This took 70 minutes, and it is thought that it may have taken fewer than 71 balls, but the results of research have not yet been published.

8. B. M. Laird scored 92 and 75 for Australia at Brisbane in 1979.

9. K. D. Walters. In the four Tests in which he played in that series, he scored 76, 118, 110, 50, 242 and 103, a sequence worthy of Bradman himself.

10. F. C. M. Alexander scored 108 at Sydney in 1961. For a batsman who never scored another century, his sequence of scores in the series of 1960–61, against a good bowling side, was remarkable. He scored 60, 5, 5, 72, 0, 108, 63 not out and 87 not out, 11 and 73 – 484 at an average of 60.67.

14. Youth

1. George Headley scored four centuries before he was 21, all in the series of 1929–30 against England. These are the only four centuries scored by a West Indies junior.

2. Kapil Dev, who had taken 87 wickets at 27.77 apiece in 23 Test matches before his 21st birthday, which fell on 6 January 1980. Second to him, but a long way behind, is Nasim-ul-Ghani, with 42 wickets at 34.88 apiece.

3. The Nawab of Pataudi, junior (otherwise Mansur Ali Khan). The circumstances were unusual and rather sad. The captain of the Indian team in the West Indies in 1961–62, N. J. Contractor, was seriously injured in the Barbados match, sustaining a fractured skull. Pataudi assumed the captaincy; at 21 years 77 days, he was the youngest Test captain from any country and all his team-mates were older than he was.

4. M. P. Bowden, who was 23 years 144 days old when he captained England against South Africa in March 1889. The team was very far from representative, and Bowden led in the second Test because the captain of the touring party, C. A. Smith, was injured.

5. Many people would guess at Hutton and Edrich, but the youngest pair were H. Gimblett and A. E. Fagg, whose combined ages on the first day of the second Test against India in 1936 totalled 42 years and 315 days. It was Fagg's first Test and Gimblett's second, and they scored 39 and 9 respectively.

6. W. H. Ashdown, who appeared for Mr G. J. V. Weigall's XI against Oxford University in June 1914, at the age of 15 years 170 days, and scored 3 and 27. It is fair to say that the match would not, under today's conventions, be granted first-class status; nevertheless Ashdown has the distinction of being the only player to have appeared in first-class cricket before the first world war and after the second, when he played for Kent.

7. D. C. S. Compton, who was 20 years 19 days old when he scored 102 against Australia at Trent Bridge in 1938.

8.   R. N. Harvey, who was 19 years 122 days when he scored 153 against India in 1948.

9.   M. W. Gatting, against Pakistan at Karachi in January 1978, when he scored 5 and 6. G. R. Dilley, against Australia at Perth in December 1979, was more successful, scoring 38 not out and 16, and taking 2 for 47 and 1 for 50.

10. The three experimental selections were D. B. Carr, who subsequently played in two Tests in India, and became secretary to the Cricket Council and the TCCB; J. G. Dewes, who played in five Tests between 1948 and 1950; and the Hon. L. R. White, who was unable to spare the time to play regularly in later years and in fact played only six first-class matches. In the Victory Test in question, none of them did very well, Dewes scoring 27 and 0, White 11 and 4, and Carr 4 and 1. This does seem to have been one of those rare occasions when English selectors erred on the side of youth.

15. Age

1. J. B. Hobbs was 46 years and 82 days old when he scored 142 for England against Australia at Melbourne in March 1929.

2. A. W. and A. D. Nourse, for South Africa. A. W. was 46 years 206 days old on the last day of his Test career, and A. D. was 40 years and 279 days.

3. Wilfred Rhodes, who played his first Test on 1 June 1899, and his last on 10 April 1930. He bowled 255 six-ball overs in his last Test series, at the age of 52.

4. Lord Harris played for Kent against the Indian touring team of 1911, at the age of 60 years and 4 months. One rather wonders whether he picked himself; it is worthy of note that eight of the ten oldest players to appear in English first-class cricket were amateurs, and four of them were the captains of the sides for which they appeared.

5. Andrew Sandham, who was 39 years and 9 months old when he scored 325 and 50 in his last Test match, against the West Indies in 1930. All the others who scored 300 or more were in their twenties at the time.

6. W. G. Grace scored 301 against Sussex at Bristol in 1896. He was 48 years old at the time, yet he batted for 8½ hours and *Wisden* says that he gave no chance – a most remarkable exhibition of concentration and stamina.

7. Sydney Barnes took 17 wickets for 159 runs against South Africa at Johannesburg in December 1913; he was 40 years old at the time. This was then a record for a bowler of any age in a Test match, and it has only been surpassed once since, by J. C. Laker's 19 for 90 at Old Trafford in 1956. Barnes set many records, not all connected with his age. He played for Wales in a first-class match at the age of 57 and, at the age of 65, he played a full season as professional for Bridgnorth and took 126 wickets at an average of 6.94. He played for

Staffordshire in the Minor Counties Championship until he was 62, and his overall record for that county is worth recording:

O	R	W	Ave.
5457.3	11,754	1441	8.15

8. W. J. O'Reilly played in one Test, against New Zealand in 1946, when he was 40. R. B. Simpson was recalled at the age of 41, in the crisis created by the setting up of World Series Cricket, and captained Australia ten times in this second career. Sir Donald Bradman's last Test ended just nine days before his fortieth birthday.

9. In 1926, J. B. Hobbs (aged 43), W. Bardsley (also aged 43) and C. G. Macartney (aged 40) all scored centuries.

10. F. J. Titmus played his first match in 1949, and his last (to date) in 1982. Others to have played in five decades include W. G. Grace, J. T. Hearne, S. F. Barnes and W. Rhodes (there are several more) while C. K. Nayudu actually played in six decades (1916–63), as did Lord Harris (1870–1911) if one reckons a decade as from, say, 1921 to 1930, which is the more correct system.

16. The numbers game (part 1)

1. Garfield Sobers made the record Test score of 365 at Kingston, Jamaica, in 1958. He went in to join Conrad Hunte at 87 for 1, facing a Pakistan score of 328. The Pakistani attack was very much handicapped. Kardar, the captain, had broken a finger on his bowling hand before the match, but managed 37 overs, and Mahmood Hussain, one of the opening bowlers, had bowled only five balls when he pulled a muscle. The main burden was carried by two men, Fazal Mahmood and Khan Mohammad, who bowled 139 overs between them. This said, Sobers and Hunte, who made 260, batted splendidly, adding 446. Sobers scored his runs in 608 minutes; West Indies declared at 790 for 3 and won by an innings and 174.

2. Gul Mahomed and V. S. Hazare added 577 for the fourth wicket for Baroda against Holkar in 1947. This remains the world record for any wicket; it surpassed the 574 added by Worrell and Walcott for Barbados against Trinidad a year earlier.

3. A. C. MacLaren made 424 for Lancashire against Somerset in 1895. It remains the record for a match in England, and seems most unlikely to be beaten in county cricket. There was then no declaration allowed on the second day of a county match, and once he had decided to bat on into the second day, Maclaren had either to play out the innings, however long it took, or instruct his batsmen to throw away their wickets. Lancashire scored 801, and had time to win by an innings.

4. J. C. Laker took 46 wickets in the England v. Australia series of 1956, the record for a series in England and also a record for all England v. Australia series. Match by match, his analyses were 6 for 87, 3 for 64, 11 for 113, 19 for 90 and 7 for 88. If rain had not ruined the first and fifth matches, he might well have topped the fifty.

5. Wilfred Rhodes took 4187 wickets at an average of 16.70 in a career lasting 33 years. He took more wickets, conceded more runs (69,993) and took 100 wickets in a season more times (23) than any other bowler.

6. D. G. Bradman scored 6996 runs in Tests, the record number by an Australian. To date he has been surpassed in aggregate terms only by G. Boycott, G. S. Sobers, M. C. Cowdrey and W. R. Hammond, but Bradman's average of 99.94 far exceeds all others.

7. S. M. Gavaskar aggregated 774 in his first Test series, in the West Indies in 1971, and this is easily the record for a debut series. Because of an injury he missed the first Test; his scores in the others were 65 and 67 not out, 116 and 64 not out, 1 and 117 not out, 124 and 220.

8. R. E. Foster scored 287 at Sydney in 1903, out of a total of 577. His score surpassed Murdoch's 211 at the Oval in 1844 as the Test record, and was not broken until Sandham made 325 at Kingston in 1930. It is still the record for an Englishman in a Test in Australia. Foster and Rhodes added 130 for the tenth wicket, still the record for an England v. Australia Test. It was Foster's first Test match and remains the highest score by a Test debutant.

9. L. Hutton scored 1294 runs in June 1949, which remains the record number of runs scored in a calendar month. He went on to score 1050 in August of that year.

10. 151 is the tenth-wicket record in Test cricket.
    B. F. Hastings (110) and R. O. Collinge (68 not out) took the New Zealand score from 251 for 9 to 402 against Pakistan in 1973, beating the 130 of Foster and Rhodes (see question 8).

17. The numbers game (part 2)

1. Hanif Mohammad scored 499 for Karachi against Bahawalpur in the semi-final of the Quaid-I-Azam Trophy in 1959. He batted for 640 minutes and hit 64 fours. Karachi scored 772 for 7 declared and won by an innings and 479 runs. Hanif's score remains the highest ever in first-class cricket.

2. S. F. Barnes took 49 wickets in the first four Tests of the 1913–14 series for England against South Africa, which remains the series record for all Test cricket. His match analyses were 10 for 105, 17 for 159, 8 for 128 and 14 for 144, and he took five or more wickets in seven of the eight innings. At this point he quarrelled with the authorities and refused to play in the final match. These were his last four Tests.

3. L. R. Gibbs took 309 wickets in Tests at an average of 29.09. This was at the time the Test record, surpassing F. S. Trueman's 307 wickets, but Gibbs has now been overtaken by D. K. Lillee. Gibbs played in 79 Tests in all.

4. D. G. Bradman scored 974 runs in the 1930 series against England, at the remarkable average of 139.14. His individual scores were 8 and 131, 254 and 1, 334, 14, and 232. His series aggregate overtook W. R. Hammond's 905 made in 1928–29, and the nearest approach since has been R. N. Harvey's 834 in 1952–53. However, two men have had high aggregates in series in which they played in four Tests only, and might well have surpassed Bradman if they had played in all five. They were S. M. Gavaskar, who made 774 in 1970–71 (see the previous quiz, question 7), and I. V. A. Richards, who made 829 in seven innings in 1976.

5. 451 is still the record Test partnership for any wicket. It was set by W. H. Ponsford (266) and D. G. Bradman (244) at the Oval in 1934. They came together at 21 for 1 on the first morning and made their runs in 316 minutes. The remarkable thing is that they had added 388 for the fourth wicket at Leeds a month earlier. That stand

lasted 341 minutes – many more overs were bowled in a day than is now the case.

6. D. C. S. Compton scored 3816 runs in 1947 at an average of 90.85, and this remains the record aggregate for an English season. He overtook T. W. Hayward, who scored 3518 in 1906; as did W. J. Edrich, also in 1947, with 3539. It does seem that Compton's record will stand for ever, unless the pattern of English cricket changes radically.

7. 561 is the world first-wicket record, set by Waheed Mirza (324) and Mansoor Akhtar (224 not out) for Karachi Whites against Quetta in 1977. The partnership lasted only 330 minutes, and both were making their maiden first-class centuries. Karachi Whites declared at the fall of the first wicket and won by an innings and 294 runs; it is permissible to wonder if the match was truly first-class.

8. G. Boycott scored 8114 runs in his Test career, the record for a player of any country. Boycott played in 108 Tests, and one wonders how many runs he would have scored if he had not withdrawn from Tests for three years, during which period England played a further 30 Tests.

9. W. R. Hammond took 78 catches in the 1928 season, the record for a fielder other than a wicket-keeper. In the course of the season he took ten catches in a match against Surrey at Cheltenham, eight of them off the bowling of C. W. L. Parker (35 of the 78 catches were off Parker's bowling).

10. 1690 is the record aggregate in a season in Australia. As one might expect, it was set by D. G. Bradman, in 1928–29. Bradman scored over 1000 runs in an Australian season 12 times, his highest average being 132.44 and his lowest 61.63.

18. Grounds

1. Test cricket has been played at the Gymkhana ground, Brabourne Stadium and Wankhede Stadium. Only the first Test of all those played in India was played at the Gymkhana, in 1933. When Test cricket returned to India in 1948–49, the Cricket Club of India had built the Brabourne, a splendid ground, though the wickets were usually slow. 25 years later, the Club and the Bombay Cricket Association fell out over the allocation of seats, and the Association took the rather extreme step of building a new ground a mile from the Brabourne, a piece of conspicuous waste if ever there was one.

2. Bangalore. West Indies beat India in the first Test played there, in November 1974.

3. Port Elizabeth, South Africa, where the first Test ever played by South Africa took place in 1889, England winning by eight wickets. South Africa's last Test, in 1970, was played on the same ground, and this time South Africa had their biggest-ever win (in terms of runs), defeating Australia by 323 runs.

4. Not surprisingly, the answer is Lord's. Ten of the matches took place before 1860, when first-class status was ill-defined, but several of them, such as North v. South in 1850, were quite indisputably great matches. The lowest-scoring match of all time was at Lord's, when MCC scored 33 and 19, the 1878 Australians 41 and 12 for 1.

5. Derbyshire, the ground being in Derby.

6. Somerset. Clarence Park is a public park in Weston-super-Mare, which is turned into a cricket ground for the annual festival, when tents, advertisements, a mobile scoreboard and so on are erected. The most sensational innings played on the ground was by M. Hyman in a minor match against Thornbury, captained by Dr E. M. Grace. Hyman scored 359, including 32 sixes!

7. The Woollongabba ground at Brisbane. The sinister undertones of the name would be appreciated by the members of most England touring sides; England played eight Tests there, from 1946 to 1974, without a victory.

8. Warwickshire. The company's ground in Coventry is used by the county at least once a year.

9. Hampshire. The ground is not named after the Test cricketer, but the benefactor who gave the ground to the people of Basingstoke.

10. Colchester, where Essex first played on the Castle Park ground, moved to the Garrison, but have now returned to the Castle Park ground, which is rather more comfortable, it is fair to say.

19. Fifty years ago

1. H. Sutcliffe and W. R. Hammond both had figures of:

I	NO	R	Ave.
9	1	440	55.00

    Sutcliffe scored 194, 1 not out, 52, 33, 9, 7, 86, 2, and 56.
    Hammond scored 112, 8, 23, 2, 85, 20, 14, 101 and 75 not
    out. England owed a good deal to their consistent batting
    in a relatively low-scoring series.

2. S. J. McCabe played a remarkable innings of 187 not out
    in the first Test at Sydney. Bradman was unfit to play in
    this match, and the other Australians could make little of
    the bodyline tactics of Larwood and Voce, who took 16
    wickets for 288 in the match. McCabe came in at 82 for 3
    and apart from him, only V. Y. Richardson (49) made runs.
    McCabe scored his 187 in some four hours, and he and
    Wall added 55 in half an hour for the tenth wicket. Wall
    scored 4 of the runs.

3. In the same match, the Nawab of Pataudi, senior, scored
    102 in his first Test innings. Curiously, K. S. Ranjitsinhji
    and K. S. Duleepsinhji, also of Indian descent, had both
    scored centuries on their first appearances against
    Australia, and Raman Subba Row was also to do so in
    1961. In spite of this success, Pataudi was out of the Test
    side by the third Test; this may have been because he was
    scoring slowly, but it has been suggested that he objected
    to participating in the bodyline attack by fielding at short
    leg.

4. Paynter, who had replaced Pataudi in the team for the
    third Test, succumbed to tonsillitis early in the fourth
    match and was thought unlikely to bat. However, the
    English batsmen got into difficulties, and Paynter rose
    from his sick-bed to score 83 in enervating heat and take
    England to a narrow first-innings lead. He had recovered
    by the second innings, and hit a six to finish the match.

5. T. W. Wall took ten for 36 in the New South Wales innings
    of 113 against South Australia at Sydney. The score-
    sheet is rather remarkable. Fingleton scored 43,

Bradman 56, and the next highest scorer was O'Reilly, with 4. Six men failed to score.

6. The great George Headley was at his best on this tour, and he scored 2320 runs at an average of 66.28. The next best West Indies batsman was B. J. Sealy, who averaged 39.70. However, Headley only came off twice in the Tests, and England had a relatively easy win.

7. Walter Hammond topped the English batting averages, making his runs at an average of 67.81. However, there were many fine batsmen about that year, the next half-dozen being: C. P. Mead 2576, average 67.78; J. B. Hobbs 1105, average 61.38; R. E. S. Wyatt 2379, average 59.47; A. Mitchell 2300, average 58.97; L. E. G. Ames 3058, average 58.80; E. Hendren 3186, average 56.89.

8. This was a most curious affair. Then, as now, the Minor Counties title was decided by a Challenge Match between the first and second counties in the Championship table. Norfolk were placed first in this table and Yorkshire 2nd XI second. They duly played, and Yorkshire won. It was later found that the result of one of Yorkshire's earlier matches had been wrongly reported and that Wiltshire, not Yorkshire, should have been placed second. It was by then too late to play a Challenge Match, and the title had to be left vacant.

9. G. O. B. Allen, who led England in the West Indies in 1947–48 at the age of 45, and J. A. Young.

10. L. N. Constantine and E. A. Martindale. The wicket was slow, and their attack was less dangerous than had been the England attack in Australia; nevertheless, they troubled most of the England batsmen until Jardine made a characteristically brave hundred.

20. Nicknames

1. The Croucher was the remarkable Gilbert Jessop, who scored 53 centuries in his first-class career, five of them double-centuries, but only once batted for more than three hours.

2. H. D. Read, who played in one Test in 1935, and W. H. V. Levett of Kent, who also played once only for England, at Calcutta in 1934, were both nicknamed Hopper, Read probably because of his action, and Levett because he came from Kent – the hop county.

3. The Essex Treasure was Walter Mead, yet another who played in just one Test, in 1899.

4. Father was still another one-Test player – C. S. Marriott, whose cricket for Kent was mostly played in the school holidays because he was a schoolmaster. He played at the Oval against the West Indies in 1933 at the age of 37, and took 11 wickets for 96.

5. Colin Milburn was nicknamed Ollie because his huge bulk put his friends in mind of the film comedian, Oliver Hardy. An immensely promising batsman, his Test career was tragically ended when he lost the sight of one eye in a motor accident.

6. Geoff Pullar, the very successful Lancashire and England batsman, was nicknamed Noddy because he could sleep anywhere and at any time.

7. Chilly was the nickname given to C. Old, formerly of Yorkshire; the derivation is obvious when you see his initial and surname together.

8. Frank Woolley of Kent, who played in 52 consecutive Tests for England and held more first-class catches than any other fielder, and Francis Ford of Middlesex were both known as Stalky because they were tall and slender. (It should be said that some connoisseurs of nicknames maintain that Ford's proper nickname was Stork.)

9. Dodger Whysall was a very successful batsman for Nottinghamshire, who played in four Tests for England and died, tragically, after a trivial accident on the dance floor.

10. The Coroner was Dr E. M. Grace, WG's elder brother, who was the secretary of Gloucestershire for 38 years.

11. Horseshoe, or Lucky, Collins captained Australia in 1924–25 and 1926. He may have been lucky as a

bookmaker (his profession) but he was far from lucky as a touring captain in 1926, missing two Tests through illness and losing a series which always looked very even.

12. Warwick Armstrong preceded Collins as Australia's captain, and was immensely successful, winning eight Tests and drawing two. A journalist described him as Leviathan – this was perhaps a touch presumptuous for Australians and, as there was a liner of that name, they preferred to call him the Big Ship.

13. Dainty was the nickname given to Bert Ironmonger in a spirit of irony. He came into the Australian side at the advanced age of 46, and although he was a very fine left-arm bowler, he was one of the worst fielders, and possibly *the* worst batsman, to have played for Australia.

14. J. J. Kelly, the successful wicket-keeper for four Australian touring teams between 1896 and 1905, was nicknamed Mother by his team-mates.

15. C. G. Macartney, who began his Test career as a spin bowler but developed, relatively late, into the outstanding attacking batsman of his day, was nicknamed the Governor-General because of his commanding style of play.

16. Ashley Mallett was nicknamed Rowdy by his team-mates in the same ironic manner as led others to call Ironmonger Dainty – Mallett was the quietest fellow breathing.

17. S. J. McCabe of Australia acquired his nickname because of a supposed resemblance to Napoleon, first noticed when the Australian cricketers were being shown round a French château.

18. Similarly, C. L. Badcock, of the 1938 Australians, had a very Italian countenance and was, naturally enough, addressed by his team-mates as Mussolini – Musso for short.

19. Froggy was A. L. Thomson, a fast bowler who played against the England tourists of 1970–71. His nickname derived from a hopping, wrong-footed bowling action, and he is not to be confused with J. R. Thomson.

20. Not all the Tigers were so called because they were ferocious: they were E. J. Smith (England), H. R. Lance (South Africa), the Nawab of Pataudi, junior (India) and W. J. O'Reilly and D. K. Lillee (Australia).

21. Figures

1. Dennis Amiss of Warwickshire and England. The highest score of 262 not out is the giveaway. This was the innings of his life, played against the West Indies at Kingston in 1974. He opened in the second innings with England 230 behind, and played what was virtually a lone hand, scoring his runs in 570 minutes out of a total of 432 for 9. He would have been the highest-scoring batsman to carry his bat through a Test innings, if Willis had got out. He scored 60.65% of the total, and only nine batsmen have scored more than 60% of a completed Test innings.

2. P. R. Umrigar, one of the half-forgotten figures of Test cricket. He played for India 59 times, scoring 12 centuries. His 223 came in the first Test ever played between India and New Zealand, at Hyderabad in 1955. His reputation among English followers of the game suffers because he had a disastrous Test series in 1952, when F. S. Trueman destroyed the Indians, but Umrigar's overall figures are highly impressive.

3. V. L. Manjrekar of India, a batsman of the same period as Umrigar. He also had a bad series in 1952; after beginning it with a century, he made 29 in his next six innings. He played on until 1965, scoring 102 not out against New Zealand in his last Test innings.

4. Bert Sutcliffe of New Zealand, who was such a good batsman that he might well have had even better figures. He did have some poor wickets to bat on, particularly in England in 1958, and was not always well supported. He had a very good tour of England in 1949, scoring 2627 runs at an average of 59.70.

5. E. J. Barlow of South Africa, who played in his country's last 30 Test matches and scored six centuries, five of them against Australia. Perhaps his greatest triumph was his 201 against Australia in 1964, when he and Graeme Pollock added 341 for the third wicket and South Africa won by ten wickets. Barlow was a good medium-pace bowler, better than his figures suggest; he was a great breaker of partnerships.

6. Roy Fredericks of the West Indies had these remarkably good figures – particularly remarkable for one who is not

usually remembered as one of the truly great. His 169 was a most brilliant innings, played against Australia at Perth in 1975; he reached his hundred in 71 balls. The equation of runs scored with balls received is the most satisfactory indicator of fast scoring, and it is a pity that we have no such details of most of the great innings of the past.

7. D. J. ('Jackie') McGlew played in 34 Tests. He was a very correct, somewhat dour opening batsman who scored seven Test hundreds, his 255 not out being against New Zealand at Wellington in 1953. In the course of it, he and A. R. A. Murray broke the world Test record for the seventh wicket, and McGlew was the second man to be on the field throughout a completed Test; the first was Nazar Mohammad, for Pakistan against India at Lucknow, just four months earlier.

8. Ian Redpath is another relatively unsung Test cricketer. He played for Australia from 1964 to 1976, scoring eight centuries. His highest score came in the first Test played at Perth, in 1970; characteristically, he went in at 17 for 3, facing an England total of 397, and saw Australia well on the way to a first-innings lead before he was out. His effort was to an extent overshadowed by Greg Chappell's century in his first Test. This seemed to be the story of Redpath's life – never a glamorous figure but always doing a good job for his side.

9. These figures belong to the great C. G. Macartney, who was an even better bat than they suggest. He began his Test career in 1907 as a slow bowler, and it was only after the first world war, at the relatively advanced age of 34, that he came to be recognised as one of the finest attacking batsmen Australia had produced. He was the second man to score a hundred before lunch on the first day of a Test, Trumper having been the first.

10. Maurice Leyland's figures stand up well in comparison with those of the other notable players on the list, the more so when we note that, of his nine centuries, seven were against Australia. He scored three in the series of 1934, and no Englishman has equalled that against Australia since then. He began his Test career with a duck, against the West Indies, and ended it with his top score of 187, in England's 903 for 7 at the Oval in 1938.

22. W. G. Grace

1. This trick question relates to an adventure undertaken by the formidable Mrs Grace, senior, in her youth. Her father was a bit of an inventor, and delighted to see what feats he could achieve with kites. On one occasion he floated his daughter across the Avon Gorge on a kitchen chair, suspended from four kites. Never let it be said that nineteenth-century maidens were all quiet and timid. Fortunately for the future of cricket, the ropes held.

2. Grace played in 22 Tests, scoring 1098 runs at an average of 32.29.

3. London County, a side which he founded and which played at Crystal Palace. It relied very much on the drawing power of Grace himself and did not long survive his retirement.

4. W. E. Midwinter, who played for Gloucestershire for some years and also played as a professional in Australia; he was in fact the first mercenary to play in two countries on a regular basis, and very strenuous it must have been. When the 1878 Australian team arrived in England, they expected Midwinter to play for them. Grace had other ideas and snatched him away from Lord's to play for Gloucestershire at the Oval. There was a furious and public row, not ended till late in the season, but the Doctor got his way – as he usually did.

5. This is false. Grace scored 54,211 runs and took 2809 wickets; Frank Woolley scored 58,959 runs and took 2068 wickets. The figures indicate what wonderful all-round cricketers both were, for only seven other players – Astill, Bailey, Hirst, Illingworth, Rhodes, Tate and Titmus – have scored as many as 20,000 runs and taken 2,000 wickets.

6. His son, WG junior, was picked to play for Cambridge University, and WG astounded his friends by appearing at Lord's in a dazzlingly smart formal outfit. His son made 40 and 28 and Cambridge won.

7. He took 17 for 89 against Nottinghamshire in 1877; he is one of only 19 bowlers to have taken 17 or more wickets in a match.

8. No. V. E. Walker scored 108 and took 10 for 74 for England v. Surrey in 1859. E. M. Grace also performed the feat, but in a match of doubtful status.

9. This is true. In 1895, Grace reached his thousand on 30 May, in his tenth innings (once not out), having played his first innings on 9 May. Don Bradman reached his thousand in nine innings (twice not out) in 1938, but had played one innings in April.

10. WG took up bowls after he had moved to London to start the London County cricket team, and captained England in the first international bowls match, in 1903.

23.   J. B. Hobbs

1. He played for Cambridgeshire in 1901 and 1904.

2. T. W. Hayward and D. R. Jardine; as it happens, he never opened for England with Andrew Sandham.

3. This rather odd statistic was created in 1920, when Hobbs bowled 83 overs and took 17 wickets at 11.82 apiece. His best days came when he opened the bowling in the absence of Rushby, taking 4 for 36 against Essex (dismissing Douglas and McGahey among others) and 5 for 21 against Warwickshire, including the formidable W. G. Quaife. As a matter of fact, Hobbs was potentially a useful medium-fast bowler, with a good action and, it need hardly be said, an intelligent approach to the task. But Surrey, understandably, preferred him to concentrate on batting.

4. Hobbs was involved in 166 century partnerships for the first wicket, including 66 with Andrew Sandham and 40 with Tom Hayward. Only Holmes and Sutcliffe have made more such partnerships than Hobbs and Sandham.

5. Hobbs agreed to play in George Duckworth's benefit match in his (Hobbs') last season – 1934. He duly made a hundred, and as he returned to the pavilion the crowd, as one man, sang 'Auld Lang Syne', Not a dry eye in the house.

6. He did this six times in all, five times in the County Championship. He held the record until 1945, when Walter Hammond achieved the feat for the seventh time. Zaheer Abbas has now overtaken Hammond, with eight 'doubles'.

7. In his great season of 1925, when he overtook W. G. Grace's total of 126 centuries, Hobbs made 16 hundreds, passing the previous record of 13, held by C. B. Fry, T. W. Hayward and E. H. Hendren. Denis Compton beat him in turn with 18 in 1947, and nobody has approached his total since.

8. 266 not out was the highest score ever made in the Gentlemen v. Players fixture. Hobbs made this score at Scarborough in 1925. He was by some margin the most successful professional batsman to appear in these fixtures, scoring 4052 runs at an average of 54.75 and 16 centuries, one more than WG.

9. This was, and remains, the highest score made at Lord's. The record stood at 278 (for MCC against Norfolk by Mr William Ward) from 1820 to 1925, when Percy Holmes made 315 not out for Yorkshire against Middlesex. His record only lasted for one year, Hobbs making his 316 not out against Middlesex in 1926.

10. Four. Two (323 and 221) with Rhodes, and two (283 and 268) with Sutcliffe.

24. Don Bradman

1. Alec Bedser dismissed him for 0 at Adelaide in 1947, bowling him with what Bradman described as the best ball ever bowled to him, an inswinger which cut away again off the seam. He did him again at Trent Bridge in 1948, Bradman being caught by Hutton at backward short leg.

2. The touring side played in Hollywood against a side raised and captained by Sir Aubrey Smith, then a noted character actor. In his youth, Smith had been a slow-medium bowler for Sussex and had captained England in the first Test ever played in South Africa. It was Smith's only Test match.

3. He hit 49 fours, but no sixes. Bradman was very little given to lifting the ball; in 1948, for example, he hit no sixes until the Festival games at the end of the season, by which time he had scored over 2000 runs in the season.

4. Eight times in all. Twice on the first day of a match (once in a Test, at Leeds in 1930) and six times on a day other than the first. The most runs he ever scored before lunch was 135; against Tasmania in 1936, he took his score from 127 to 262.

5. He made the record number of 37 scores over 200. Twelve of these were in Tests, 8 each for New South Wales and South Australia, 7 for Australian teams in England in games other than Tests, and 2 in testimonial games in Australia. His percentage of hundreds which he went on to turn into double-hundreds (31.62) is much higher than that of any other batsman who has had a career of comparable length.

6. Bradman was *never* out in the nineties in a Test; his highest double-figure score was 89, at Lord's in 1948. This statistic may say more than any other about his temperament.

7. Hedley Verity got him out eight times in 27 innings in which he bowled at him. But it would be wrong to assume that even Verity was Bradman's master, for he did make eight hundreds in those 27 innings.

8. He reached 1000 on 27 May 1938, in his ninth innings of the season. To that point he had not been bowled, and it is said that he had not given an unaccepted chance.

9. All the Australian players had signed contracts which forbade them to write anything for publication during the tour. Bradman was writing an autobiography at the time, and some extracts were published, by agreement between his publishers and a newspaper, before the tour ended. £50 of Bradman's bonus was accordingly withheld.

10. Only two. J. Ryder and W. M. Woodfull.

25.   Walter Hammond

1. At Dover. This gave rise to a nasty little controversy, when Kent objected to his playing for Gloucestershire on a doubtful residential qualification, and he lost a season's cricket. The qualification rules were strictly enforced at that time.

2. Hammond played his first match against Lancashire at Cheltenham in 1920, and Richard Tyldesley dismissed him lbw for 0. He was to compensate the Cheltenham spectators in due course.

3. At Johannesburg, in Christmas week 1927. He started well, scoring 51 and taking five wickets in an innings.

4. 5 for 36, in the match referred to in the answer to question 3. His victims included H. W. Taylor and R. H. Catterall, perhaps South Africa's two best batsmen at the time.

5. 9 for 23, at Cheltenham in 1928. This was part of the greatest all-round week any cricketer can ever have enjoyed. Against Surrey he scored 139 and 143, held ten catches in the match, which remains the world record, and dismissed Hobbs. Then against Worcestershire he took 9 for 23, catching the other batsman off Parker, scored 80, and took 6 for 105 in the second innings. (See the answer to question 2.)

6. He hit ten sixes during his 336 not out at Auckland in 1933, and this is a record which may stand for some time, unless Botham has a day out on a small ground.

7. In the last Test played before the second world war, Hammond joined Hutton at 77 for 2 in the second innings, with England still 69 behind. They almost played out time, Hammond being out for 138 shortly before the close. Hutton scored 165 not out.

8. He headed the averages eight times in succession, from 1933 to 1946 (if we ignore the very brief 1945 season). In those eight seasons he scored 20,937 runs at an average of 65.43.

9. He scored seven double-centuries in Tests, four against Australia, two (in successive innings) against New Zealand, and one against India.

10. He made three scores of over 300 in county cricket, the highest being 317 against Nottinghamshire in 1936.

26. Len Hutton

1. He scored 19 centuries in all, five each against Australia and the West Indies, four against South Africa, three against New Zealand and two against India. (He only played twice against Pakistan.) It is entirely typical of him that his best performances were against the most formidable opposition.

2. 205, against the West Indies at Kingston in 1954. This was a momentous performance. England had lost the first two Tests, won the third (Hutton scoring 169) and drawn the fourth, so they needed to win the fifth to share the series. Bailey bowled West Indies out on the first day for 139, and Hutton finished them off with this innings, the first double-century by an England captain in an overseas Test.

3. 1949. This is the fourth highest aggregate on record. Hutton averaged 68.58.

4. 280 not out, scored for Yorkshire against Hampshire in 1939. For a man who at this stage of his career was reckoned a dour player, Hutton wasted little time. He scored his runs in 375 minutes, out of a total of 493 for 1 declared, and then took 4 for 40 in the Hampshire second innings.

5. Surprisingly, at Scarborough, where his record was:

I	NO	R	HS	Ave.
78	8	4190	241	59.85

6. Less surprisingly, at the Oval, his record being:

I	NO	R	HS	Ave.
19	2	1521	364	89.47

    He scored a triple-century and two double-centuries at the Oval, and his is the second highest aggregate by one player on one ground in Tests; Bradman scored 1671 runs at Melbourne.

7. J. H. Parks of Sussex, who could perhaps be counted unlucky. Both were playing in their first Test, and Hutton scored 0 and 1, Parks 22 and 7; Hutton went on to score

6971 Test runs, but Parks never played for England again.

8. Herbert Sutcliffe. Hutton batted at no. 5 in his first match for Yorkshire, against Cambridge University, and was run out for 0. In his second match against Oxford, he batted at no. 6 and was out for 5, but in the second innings he opened with Sutcliffe and scored 57 not out.

9. Hutton and Cyril Washbrook scored 359 for the first wicket against South Africa at Johannesburg in 1948, Hutton scoring 158 and Washbrook 195.

10. Hutton and Sutcliffe twice scored 315 for the first wicket, once in the match against Hampshire already referred to in the answer to question 4 (Sutcliffe scoring 116), and once against Leicestershire on his twenty-first birthday, in 1937. On this occasion Hutton scored 153 and Sutcliffe 189.

27. Garfield Sobers

1. Sobers was 17 years and 245 days old when he first played in a Test, at Kingston in 1954. Really accurate details of the age of some players are hard to come by, but there have probably been four Test players under the age of 17 – Mushtaq Mohammad, Aftab Baloch, Nasim-ul-Ghani and Khalid Hassan, all of Pakistan. Sobers is the second youngest West Indian Test player, the youngest being J. E. D. Sealy.

2. He scored 365 not out in his seventeenth Test and his twenty-ninth innings. Curiously enough, R. B. Simpson of Australia also scored a 300 as his maiden Test century; he scored 311 in his thirtieth Test and his fifty-second innings.

3. Sobers scored 824 for six times out in the series of 1957–58 against Pakistan; this included not only his record score of 365 not out but a century in each innings of the next Test.

4. This is true. He scored 7041 runs for Nottinghamshire at an average of 48.89, and 8032 runs in Tests at an average of 57.78. His Test record is also better than his first-class career average of 54.87.

5. This also relates to the match at Kingston in which he set his Test record of 365 not out. He and C. C. Hunte, who scored 260, put on 446 for the second wicket. This is the fourth highest second-wicket stand in first-class cricket, and the second highest stand for any wicket in a Test, the highest being to the credit of D. G. Bradman and W. H. Ponsford, who added 451, also for the second wicket, at the Oval in 1934.

6. 109, which places him fourth on the all-time list of fielders, behind Cowdrey (120), R. B. Simpson and Hammond (110 each). Greg Chappell, on 106 at the time of writing, will probably have overtaken him by publication of this book.

7. South Australia, for whom he played from 1961 to 1964, scoring 2707 runs in three seasons at an average of 62.95, and taking 137 wickets at an average of 26.02.

8. 174, at Leeds in 1966. By his standards he was not very successful for the West Indies in England, if the scoring of centuries is taken as the measure. He 'only' scored five Test centuries on five tours, but his average of 53.2 for Tests in England would have satisfied most players; he also took 62 wickets.

9. Lance Gibbs, off whom he took the extraordinary number of 39 catches.

10. At Georgetown, where he scored 125 and 109 not out against Pakistan in 1958, in the match already referred to in the answer to question 3.

28.   Ian Botham

1. He was born at Heswall, in Cheshire.

2. This performance came in a Benson and Hedges Cup quarter-final against Hampshire in June 1974. Hampshire made 182, and when the 18-year-old Botham came in, Somerset were 113 for 7. Soon afterwards he was felled by a bouncer from Andy Roberts, losing four teeth. In a royal rage he hit 45 not out in 14 overs and Somerset won by one wicket.

3. He took 5 for 74 in the Australian first innings at Nottingham in 1977, dismissing Greg Chappell, Walters, Marsh, Walker and Thomson.

4. This is false. He went on tour in the winter of 1977–78 and was left out of the three Tests against Pakistan. He returned against New Zealand, scored 212 runs and took 17 wickets in a three-match series, and has not been omitted since.

5. He reached this target in his twenty-first Test, beating the record of M. H. ('Vinoo') Mankad, who had done so in 23 Tests.

6. This is false. Botham was the first (and so far the only) man to score a century and take ten wickets in the same Test – he did this at Bombay in the Silver Jubilee Test in 1980, scoring 114 and taking 6 for 58 and 7 for 48. Alan Davidson had preceded him in the tied Test played at Brisbane in 1960, scoring 44 and 80 and taking 5 for 135 and 6 for 87.

7. Botham scored 228 against Gloucestershire at Taunton in 1980, batting for 184 minutes and hitting ten sixes and 27 fours.

8. He took a hat-trick on the first day of the 1978 season at Lord's, for MCC against Middlesex, the joint champions of 1977.

9. Botham came on to bowl at 105 for five (Australia needing to make 149 to win) and took five wickets for one run in 28 balls.

10. Coming together at 135 for 7 when England still needed to make 92 runs to make Australia bat again, they added 117 runs. The last two wickets put on a further 104 runs, and the rest is history.

29.   The Chappells

1. Greg Chappell held 14 catches in the six-Test series against England in 1974–75, second only to the 15 catches held by Jack Gregory in the five Tests of 1920–21.

2. In that same series, Greg held seven catches at Perth, the record for a fielder in a single Test. Yajuvendra Singh also held seven catches against England at Bangalore in 1977. It is a curiosity that Yajuvendra Singh held five catches in one innings in that Test, and shares this record with Chappell's grandfather, Vic Richardson, who achieved the feat in his last Test, at Durban in 1936.

3. W. M. Lawry, captain of the 1969–70 team which toured South Africa, so described Ian Chappell. Chappell scored 92 runs for eight times out in the series, including three ducks.

4. Three times. In 1972, Greg scored 113 and Ian 118 against England at the Oval; in 1973, Greg scored 106 in the first innings and Ian 106 not out in the second innings against the West Indies at Bridgetown; and in 1974, Greg scored 247 not out and 133 and Ian 145 and 121 against New Zealand at Wellington.

5. Rodney Marsh. He has also played under Ian Chappell in every Test in which *he* captained Australia. The total period runs from 1971 to 1982, with an interregnum during the World Series Cricket dispute, during which R. B. Simpson, G. N. Yallop and K. J. Hughes captained, and S. J. Rixon, J. A. Maclean and K. J. Wright kept wicket.

6. Two, both for the third wicket. They put on 264 in the match at Wellington already referred to in the answer to question 4 and 201 at the Oval in 1972.

7. 196, against Pakistan in 1972. This remained the highest score in Australia v. Pakistan matches until Greg Chappell scored 235 at Faisalabad in 1980.

8. He took 5 for 61 in a rather unusual match against Pakistan at Sydney in 1973. Australia scored 334, and when Pakistan batted Lillee was able to bowl only ten overs because of a back injury. Chappell rose to the occasion and took his 5 for 61 in 18.6 overs. Pakistan were all out for 360 and Australia fell into trouble, collapsing to 101 for 8, only 75 ahead. However, J. R. Watkins, playing in his only Test, added 83 with R. A. L. Massie and it proved just enough. Lillee was able to bowl in the second innings, and he and Walker bowled Pakistan out for 106 to win a remarkable victory.

9. Ian Chappell has played under four captains. R. B. Simpson, W. M. Lawry, B. N. Jarman (in one Test) and his brother Greg.

10. This is true. He has captained in 42 Tests, the next highest Australian total being R. B. Simpson's 39.

30. Wicket-keepers

1. This kind of record depends on two things; the careers of bowler and 'keeper have to coincide pretty exactly, and the bowler has to be of the type to induce chances to the 'keeper. The chances have still to be taken, though. Dennis Lillee and Rodney Marsh lead the field, Marsh having taken 88 catches off Lillee. Bob Taylor has taken 52 catches off Ian Botham, and Wally Grout caught 44 and stumped 1 off Alan Davidson.

2. John Murray, who overtook Herbert Strudwick's career aggregate of 1491 dismissals in 1975 and went on to a total of 1526 before retiring at the end of the season. Bob Taylor overtook Murray's figure in the first match of England's 1982–83 tour of Australia, playing against Queensland.

3. Bert Oldfield, who caught 78 batsmen and stumped 52, was the only pre-war keeper to exceed the hundred. His figure of 52 stumpings (28 of them off Grimmett) seems likely to stand for ever.

4. Leslie Ames dismissed 127 batsmen in 1929, 121 in 1928 and 100 in 1932. He owed a great deal to A. P. ('Tich') Freeman, off whom he made a vast number of stumpings.

5. This record stands to the credit of the remarkable Godfrey Evans, who conceded no byes in the second or third Tests of the 1946–47 series while Australia were scoring 659 for 8 declared and 365. The 659 was the second highest total in first-class cricket to contain no byes. The highest was 672 for 7 declared, A. P. Wickham being the wicket-keeper for Somerset against Hampshire in 1899.

6. A. T. W. ('Wally') Grout held eight catches for Queensland against Western Australia in 1959–60. Nine players have held seven catches in an innings, Bob Taylor doing so three times. Derek Taylor of Somerset held eight catches in a Benson and Hedges match against the Combined Universities in 1982.

7. W. H. Brain, who stumped three batsmen off C. L. Townsend, playing for Gloucestershire against Somerset in 1893.

8. Leslie Ames, as the answer to question 4 may have indicated. Most reference books give his number of stumpings as 415; modern research may revise this, but he certainly stumped more than 400 batsmen. Those who follow him on this list are F. H. Huish, David Hunter and E. Pooley.

9. D. T. Lindsay of South Africa, in the remarkable first Test of the 1966–67 series against Australia. South Africa opened with 199, and Australia replied with 325, Lindsay taking his six catches. Lindsay came in at 268 for 5 in the second innings and hit 182 in 3½ hours, including five sixes. South Africa then bowled Australia out for 261 and won by 233 runs. Lindsay went on to score 606 runs in the series (the most ever by a wicket-keeper) and make 24 catches.

10. Arnold Long, for Surrey against Sussex in 1964. Curiously, he made two catches off the bowling of Geoff Arnold, and one off Stewart Storey, and all three moved to Sussex in due course.

31. True or false?

1. This is true; it happened twice. At Durban in 1910, N. C. Tufnell was allowed to keep for England after Strudwick had been injured, and rewarded the chivalrous South African captain (S. J. Snooke) by stumping him off G. J. Thompson. At Lahore in 1965, B. E. Congdon took over when A. E. Dick was unfit and stumped Pervez Sajjad off the bowling of B. W. Sinclair. Sinclair was having his only spell with the ball in 21 Tests, and took 2 for 32.

2. This also is true. The greatest number of catches taken in a season by a fielder is 78, taken by W. R. Hammond in 1928; the most by a wicket-keeper is 96, by J. G. Binks in 1960.

3. Also true. One player, L. Hutton, has been out 'obstructing the field' and three, W. R. Endean, A. M. J. Hilditch and Mohsin Khan, have been out 'handled the ball', but 'hit the ball twice' remains the only way in which no Test batsman has yet been out.

4. This is false. Grace is the only man to be out for a 'pair' in his only Test for England, but C. I. J. Smith and G. A. Gooch were also out for 'pairs' in their first Test matches in 1935 and 1975 respectively.

5. False. Four batsmen have done so, in every case in June and August. They are C. B. Fry (1901), K. S. Ranjitsinhji (1899), H. Sutcliffe (1932) and L. Hutton (1949). This is rather surprising, as 1000 runs has only been scored in a month 36 times in all.

6. False. Hayward achieved the feat in 1904 and again in 1906, but four players had preceded him – K. S. Ranjitsinhji (1899 and 1900), R. Abel, C. B. Fry and J. T. Tyldesley (all in 1901).

7. True. On 11 January 1930, England teams were playing in Christchurch and in Bridgetown. In point of fact, it rained all day in Christchurch and no play actually took place, but there was play on both grounds on 13 January. Because of the time difference, play was not actually

taking place simultaneously. Two England teams played Tests in the same overseas season in 1891–92, but Tests did not take place on the same day.

8. True. John Wisden, playing for the North v. the South in 1850, bowled all ten batsmen, and W. E. Hollies, playing for Warwickshire against Nottinghamshire in 1946, bowled seven and had three lbw.

9. False. Hedley Verity did this when he took 10 for 10 against Nottinghamshire in 1932.

10. True. John Langridge scored eight double-centuries, all for Sussex in the County Championship. T. F. Shepherd is next on this particular list, with five double-centuries.

32. Middlesex

1. In 1936 and 1936–37, G. O. B. Allen captained six Test teams of which R. W. V. Robins was a member. Robins himself became England captain in 1937, but Allen did not play under his captaincy.

2. M. W. W. Selvey, who took 101 wickets in 1978.

3. E. H. ('Patsy') Hendren, who took 562 catches between 1907 and 1937. We are rather apt to think of Hendren as a dashing outfield with a fine throw, but he was also a most accomplished slip and close catcher in what we would describe today as the 'bat-pad' position, and most of his catches were held close to the bat. He was a great all-round fieldsman.

4. J. D. B. Robertson scored 331 not out for Middlesex against Worcestershire at Worcester in 1949. This was not only the highest score ever made for Middlesex, and Robertson's own highest score, but the fourth highest score ever made in a single day and the highest score made in England since Hutton's 364 at the Oval in 1938. Edrich and Compton were absent on Test duty, but Robertson was strongly supported by Dewes, Mann, Allen and Robins; the last two were 46 and 43 years old respectively.

5. G. O. B. Allen, already mentioned, took 10 wickets for 40 against Lancashire in 1929. His performance was the more remarkable in that he hit the wicket eight times and bowled four men for ducks. Nevertheless, Lancashire led by 13 on the first innings and had rather the better of a draw. Harry Lee of Middlesex scored 124 out of 228, and 105 not out in a total of 170 for 5.

6. Lord Dunglass, later to become in turn the 14th Earl of Home, Sir Alec Douglas-Home and Baron Home of the Hirsel, played three matches for Middlesex in 1924 and 1925, scoring 23 runs and taking four wickets.

7. These remarkable innings were to the credit of C. I. J. ('Jim') Smith. Against Kent in 1935, he scored 50 in 14 minutes, hitting four sixes, six fours and two singles, and

against Gloucestershire in 1938, he reached his 50 in 11 minutes, with six sixes, two fours, two twos and two singles. His time for the fifty on this occasion remained the record until C. C. Inman beat it in 1965, being fed with full tosses to bring about a declaration. His fifty came in 11 scoring strokes, a record he shares with five other players.

8. Playing against North-Eastern Transvaal on the 1948–49 tour, Denis Compton went from 120, his overnight score, to 300 in an hour and a half.

9. P. R. Downton, playing against Kent at Lord's in 1980, scored 160 for the first wicket with J. M. Brearley and, in the second innings, 109 with K. P. Tomlins. It was Downton's first game for Middlesex, and he was playing against his former county.

10. A. N. Connolly, capped in 1969. (J. R. Thomson played for Middlesex in 1981, but was not capped.)

33. Surrey

1. 811, against Somerset in 1899. This is the second
   highest total ever in the County Championship, and the
   fourth highest ever made in England. Bobby Abel carried
   his bat for 357, and the side's score of 811 is the greatest
   number of runs ever scored while one batsman was at
   the wicket.

2. Tom Richardson took 1775 wickets for Surrey at an
   average of 17.87. Many of Richardson's feats border on
   the miraculous. In all first-class matches in the four
   seasons of 1894–97 he took 1005 wickets at an average
   of 14.08, and in only 14 Test matches he took 88 wickets,
   including five or more wickets in an innings no fewer
   than eleven times. His exhibitions of stamina would have
   been remarkable in a slow bowler, but he was one of the
   fastest of his generation.

3. They were fifth in 1969, the first season of the League,
   and again in 1980.

4. C. T. A. Wilkinson, captain in 1914, 1919 and 1920,
   played for England in the Olympics.

5. M. J. Stewart and J. H. Edrich, who opened together in
   two Tests in 1963, against the West Indies.

6. Roy Swetman, who kept in eleven Tests in 1959 and
   1960. He did reasonably well but was supplanted by
   J. M. Parks, a better batsman.

7. Surridge captained Surrey in the five seasons from 1952
   to 1956, and won the Championship every time. Surridge
   was not a great player himself (his batting average was
   13.01 and his bowling average 29.64) but he was a
   superb field and an inspiring and inspired captain.

8. P. B. H. May, who scored 85 centuries in his relatively
   brief career. He is followed on the Surrey list by
   K. F. Barrington with 76 hundreds and R. Abel with 74.

9. A. Marshal of Queensland.

10. 706 for 4 declared, which is in fact the highest by any county since the war. It came in the Bank Holiday match at Nottingham in 1947. The home team batted first and scored 401, with no centuries and only two fifties – a most consistent display. D. G. W. Fletcher, in only his second county match, scored 194 for Surrey, and H. S. Squires 154. Then on the third morning, J. F. Parker and E. R. T. Holmes both scored centuries before lunch – a rare but not unique feat. Notts drew the game by scoring 201 for 4.

34. Yorkshire

1. Maurice Leyland, who had a remarkable first match at Melbourne in 1929, scoring 137 and 53 not out; England still lost. His last Test against Australia was the famous Oval Test of 1938, in which he scored 187 and added 382 for the second wicket with Len Hutton.

2. Herbert Sutcliffe is not usually thought of as a mighty hitter, but he could hit when in the mood. At Kettering in 1933, he hit ten sixes in an innings of 113; there was a very short boundary on one side, over which he was able to hit Jupp's off-breaks. It was an extraordinary match, since Northamptonshire were dismissed for 27 and 68, Macaulay taking 11 for 34, and only four men, all Yorkshiremen, got past 30. Seen in this light, Sutlciffe's hitting is all the more remarkable.

3. J. V. Wilson, who was picked for the 1954–55 tour as insurance in case Compton's injured knee failed him (it didn't). Wilson didn't have a particularly good tour with the bat and was permanent twelfth man for the Tests, in which he held two catches. He had only a reasonable season in 1955, was not picked for England, and his chance was gone.

4. W. E. Harbord, a Yorkshire amateur, went on the 1934–35 tour of the West Indies with no particular form to recommend him. He did little in the few games he had on the tour, and was probably never considered for the Test team. His career for Yorkshire was pretty undistinguished; he played 20 innings between 1929 and 1935, averaging 20.55, and did not bowl.

5. Arthur Wood, in the Oval Test of 1938. He went on to play in three more Tests in 1939.

6. J. G. Binks made 412 consecutive Championship appearances between 1955 and 1969. Only K. G. Suttle, with 423 consecutive matches, has bettered him, but in a way Binks' record is the more remarkable, wicket-keepers being perhaps more prone to injury than other players.

7. Sir Leonard Hutton, who played in 79 Tests and scored 6971 runs at an average of 56.57, and his son Richard, who played five times, scored 219, average 36.50 and took nine wickets at an average of 28.55.

8. David Hunter, who must be one of the best wicket-keepers to have missed a Test cap. He played from 1888 to 1909, catching 955 batsmen and stumping 372.

9. Martyn Moxon aged 21, who scored 116 when Yorkshire followed on against Essex at Leeds and played a major part in saving the match. The last Yorkshireman to score a hundred on debut before Moxon was C. Tyson, who did so in 1921.

10. Alonzo Drake, who performed this feat against Somerset at Weston-super-Mare, bowling unchanged throughout the match with Major Booth. It seemed that the two would be the mainstay of Yorkshire's bowling for years, but before play was resumed after the war both were dead; Booth had been killed in action and Drake had died of heart disease.

35. Lancashire

1. Cyril Washbrook, who had last played for England in 1951, was one of the selectors in 1956. The England batting failed at Lord's, and with England one down with three to play, his fellow-selectors persuaded him to play at Leeds. He went in to bat at 17 for 3 on the first morning and scored 98. The match, and the next one, were won by superb spin bowling by J. C. Laker, but without Washbrook the recovery would not have been possible.

2. Also in 1956, when Lancashire beat Leicestershire at Old Trafford. The first day was washed out and on the second Leicestershire were bowled out for 108. A. Wharton and J. Dyson scored 166 for the first wicket, at which point Geoff Edrich, the deputy captain, declared. Leicestershire failed again, being all out for 122, and Wharton and Dyson knocked off the runs.

3. R. G. Barlow, who did so against Nottinghamshire in 1882. The side's total score was 69, and at one point Barlow batted for 80 minutes without adding to his score.

4. This occurred in 1971, when Lancashire played Kent. Lancashire made 224 for 7 in their 60 overs, and Kent were 197 for 6 with six overs to go when Asif Iqbal, who had made 89 in 2¼ hours, drove the ball to extra cover and J. Bond, the Lancashire captain, made a wonderful falling catch. The last three Kent wickets fell for three runs, and Lancashire had won.

5. David Lloyd, who scored 214 not out against India at Birmingham in 1974. The only other Lancashire player to score 200 for England is E. Paynter, who did so twice.

6. C. H. Parkin, who played in the Test at Edgbaston in which Gilligan and Tate dismissed South Africa for 30. South Africa made 309 in the follow-on and Parkin bowled only 16 overs. He, or more probably his ghost, wrote a piece in a newspaper suggesting that he ought to have been used more, and he was not picked again.

7. L. O. S. Poidevin and A. Kermode, who added 142 against Sussex at Eastbourne in 1907.

8. F. C. Hayes, playing against Glamorgan at Swansea in 1977. He was batting against M. A. Nash, who was also the sufferer when G. S. Sobers hit 36 off an over, the only time Hayes' feat has been beaten.

9. K. Cranston, against South Africa in 1947.

10. W. E. Phillipson and W. B. Roberts. Both might well have played in Tests had they been just a little luckier. Phillipson was an all-rounder who scored 4050 runs for Lancashire at an average of 25.96 and took 545 wickets at 24.78 apiece. Roberts was a slow left-arm bowler who took 382 wickets at 20.86.

36. Kent

1. S. H. Day, who scored 101 not out for Kent against Gloucestershire in 1897, while still at Malvern.

2. M. C. Cowdrey, who led the county from 1957 to 1971. Kent had been second in 1967 and 1968. Kent's previous win had been in 1913, the climax of a remarkable spell of six seasons in which they were first three times, second twice and third once. In those six years they won 103 matches, lost 20 and drew 33.

3. Seven times. They won the Gillette Cup in 1967 and 1974, and were runners-up in 1971. They won the Benson and Hedges Cup in 1973, 1976 and 1978, and were runners-up in 1977.

4. Most surprisingly, this record stands to the credit not of Frank Woolley, who took more catches than any other fielder in the history of the game, nor of Colin Cowdrey, a very high-class slip-fielder, but of Chris Tavaré, who held 48 catches in 1978, when fewer county matches were played than in Woolley's day. Tavaré played in only 24 matches, and his average of two catches per match represents quite an achievement.

5. Kent made the remarkable score of 803 for 4 declared against Essex at Brentwood in 1934, the third highest score ever made in the County Championship. W. H. Ashdown scored 332 in 6¼ hours, adding 352 for the second wicket with Wolley and 245 for the third with Ames, who scored 202 not out in 170 minutes. Students of over-rates may like to note that Essex sent down 146.2 overs in the seven hours of the innings.

6. A. P. Freeman performed this amazing feat in three different seasons: 1930, when he took 260 wickets and 13 other bowlers took 212 between them; 1931 (Freeman 257, 15 others 197); and 1933 (Freeman 262, 18 others 229). In 1932 Freeman took 226 wickets and the rest 250, so in four consecutive seasons, Freeman took 1005 wickets for Kent while the other bowlers, 26 of them in all, were taking 888. Good going for a middle-aged man – he was born in 1888.

7. E. Humphreys, who played for Kent from 1899 to 1920, scoring 15,308 runs and taking 306 wickets.

8. The Hearnes, Alec and George, who played for England, and Frank, who played both for England and South Africa. In the Test at Cape Town in 1892, all three played, Frank representing South Africa. Their second cousin, J. T. Hearne of Middlesex, also played for England in this match.

9. A. W. Catt, playing against Northamptonshire in 1955. He was suffering from sunburn, which impeded his free movement, and one wonders why his captain did not replace him with a fitter player. But the captain in question, Doug Wright, was himself a very difficult bowler to take, and perhaps none of the other players fancied the job.

10. Arthur Fagg, umpiring in the England v. West Indies match at Edgbaston in 1973, took exception to the West Indians' attitude when he gave Boycott not out, and declined to stand at the beginning of the third day's play. Alan Oakman, the Warwickshire coach and a former first-class umpire, took his place, but after one over Fagg, having made his point, resumed duty.

37. Nottinghamshire

1. R. J. Hadlee took 105 wickets at an average of 14.89, E. E. Hemmings 84 at 20.71, and C. E. B. Rice 65 at 19.20.

2. An oddity, this. W. W. Keeton scored 312 not out against Middlesex in 1939, but at Kennington Oval. The reason the two counties were playing at the Oval was not, as may be supposed, that the war had broken out or was about to break out. Lord's was required for the Eton and Harrow match, the rights of the landlord (MCC) taking precedence over those of the tenant (Middlesex).

3. Thomas L. ('Tich') Richmond, who played for Notts from 1912 to 1922, taking 1176 wickets. He was picked against the Australians at Trent Bridge in 1921, but was no more successful than most of the other players who appeared for England that year, taking 2 for 86.

4. Copley was a member of the Notts ground-staff in 1930 and was called upon to substitute for England on the last day of the Trent Bridge Test, both Sutcliffe and Larwood being off the field. He made a spectacular catch to dismiss McCabe; it was a major factor in England's win, their only one of the series. Copley played only one game for Notts in his career, scoring 7 runs for twice out and taking no wickets.

5. A. W. Carr, who captained in the first four Tests of the 1926 series against Australia before being replaced by A. P. F. Chapman for the last Test in circumstances which remain somewhat mysterious: the selectors announced that he was unfit, but there is a school of thought which maintains that it was a diplomatic illness. Carr's four Tests had been drawn, but England won the fifth and Chapman, not Carr, was the man who regained the Ashes. Later, Carr led England in two Tests against South Africa in 1929, winning one and drawing one, but no Notts man has been captain since.

6. George Gunn, who had a successful tour in 1911–12, and was not selected again until 1930, when he played in all four Tests on England's tour of the West Indies and became the fourth oldest Test player of all time. (The

oldest, Wilfred Rhodes, played his last Test in the same game as Gunn did so.) It is said that Gunn was invited to go on the 1920–21 tour of Australia but left the letter, unopened, in his pocket all winter. I do not know that the story is true, but if it were, it would be typical of Gunn and his approach to life and to cricket, which he could never take wholly seriously.

7. Harold Larwood, playing in what turned out to be his last Test, in 1933, was sent in at no. 4, probably to preserve him for bowling rather than to protect a batsman. It is said that he rather resented this and laid about him in a rage; he certainly played a brilliant innings, scoring his 98 in 135 minutes.

8. F. C. Matthews, a fairly obscure player, took 17 for 89 against Northamptonshire in 1923. W. G. Grace obtained the same figures for Gloucestershire at Cheltenham in 1877.

9. H. J. Butler, who had existed in the shadow of Larwood and Voce before the war but was now having something of an Indian summer. He took 7 for 66 in his first Test at Leeds, went to the West Indies that winter and took five wickets in his only Test there. He dismissed, among others Weekes (twice), Nourse (twice) and Mitchell. His nickname? 'Penelope'.

10. W. W. Whysall, nicknamed 'Dodger'. Another player to enjoy an Indian summer, Whysall scored 2028 for Notts in 1927, 2573 in 1928, 2620 in 1929 and 2151 in 1930. Later in 1930, he had a fall on the dance floor and died of septicaemia at the age of 43.

38.   Some great Test players

1. Neil Harvey was the second Australian to reach his 5000 runs in Tests; Don Bradman was the first. Harvey passed 5000 in his sixty-first Test, at Delhi, and went on to an aggregate of 6149 at an average of 48.41. He scored 21 centuries, six of them against England and eight, in two series, against South Africa.

2. Jack Hobbs scored 3636 runs against Australia at an average of 54.26. He hit 12 centuries against Australia, the last coming in his last Test in Australia, when he was 46. This score was made at Melbourne, where he scored 1178 runs; he is the only batsman to have scored over 1000 runs on one ground away from his own country.

3. Colin Cowdrey, who scored 2433 against Australia, 1751 against the West Indies, 1133 against New Zealand and 1021 against South Africa.

4. Surprisingly perhaps, this record stands not to Don Bradman but to Walter Hammond who, in his 336 not out against New Zealand at Auckland in 1933, reached his 300 in 287 minutes. Bradman's best time was 336 minutes at Leeds in 1930. Hammond hit ten sixes and 33 fours.

5. Don Bradman, who scored 1671 runs at Melbourne at an average of 128.54. His sequence of scores is worth recording; it was 79, 112, 123, 37 not out, 152, 2, 167, 0, 103 not out, 13, 270, 169, 79, 49, 132, 127 not out and 57 retired hurt.

6. Clarrie Grimmett, who took 23 wickets for 1024 runs in the 1928–29 series. His analyses were 3–167, 6–131, 2–191, 2–114, 2–96, 5–102, 1–117, 0–40 and 2–66. In the next series, in 1930, he took 29 wickets for 925 runs – always plenty of action when he was playing.

7. Garfield Sobers, who took 235 wickets at 34.03 apiece. This is by no means as bad as it seems; he often bowled when batting was easy and the other bowlers had been mastered. He also batted a bit!

8. This was the somewhat fanciful nickname given to the graceful Brian Statham. He preferred to be called George.

9. Richie Benaud had an excellent season in South Africa in 1957–58, taking 106 wickets at an average of 19.39. The following year, he took 82 wickets at 19.25 apiece in Australia. In average terms, Benaud's performance was less impressive than that of Sydney Barnes who, in 1913–14, took 104 wickets at an average of 10.74.

10. Bishen Bedi achieved these figures in a Ranji Trophy match for Delhi against Jammu and Kashmir in 1974. He had taken 6 for 29 in the first innings, so his match figures were 13 for 34. By a curious coincidence, P. K. Shivalkar, another slow left-arm bowler, who was only kept out of the Indian side by Bedi, also had a best match performance of 13 for 34 in a Ranji Trophy match, and R. Goel, a third slow left-armer and a contemporary of the other two, has a best performance of 13 for 29, also against Jammu and Kashmir.

39. Some great Test matches

1. This was 'Jessop's match', the fifth Test at the Oval in
    1902. Australia batted first and made 324, to which
    England replied with 183 (Trumble 8 for 65). On a
    bowlers' wicket, Australia were out for 121 and England
    were set 263 to win. When Jessop went in they were 48
    for 5, and it was at this point that he played his deathless
    innings. Even then, it took a ninth-wicket stand of 34
    between Hirst and Lilley, and a final stand of 15 from
    Hirst and Rhodes, to see England to a one-wicket win.

2. At Leeds in 1948, England made 496 and 365 for 8
    declared. Australia, who had scored 458 in the first
    innings, were set 404 to win in just under six hours.
    Fortunately for them, England had a very ill-balanced
    attack and were not having a good day in the field. Morris
    scored 182 and Bradman 173 not out, and Australia won
    by seven wickets.

3. This refers to the classic match at Lord's in 1930.
    England made 425, mostly on the first day. They rather
    threw their wickets away towards the end, but they had
    not realised that the extension of Tests to four days, and
    Bradman's phenomenal speed of scoring, meant that
    400 was far from a safe score any more. Bradman made
    254 and Woodfull 155 as Australia totalled 729 for 6.
    England put up a tough fight, scoring 375, but Australia
    had plenty of time to win. It is worth remarking that 505
    overs were bowled in less than four days.

4. This markable feat is to the credit of Trevor Bailey, the
    occasion being the fifth Test at Kingston, Jamaica, in
    1954. The West Indies were out for 139 soon after tea on
    the first day, Bailey having taken 7 for 34 in 16 overs. He
    had opened the batting in the previous Test, Hutton's
    specialist partners not having risen to the occasion, and
    he now did so again, seeing out the evening and scoring
    23. Bailey opened in quite a few subsequent Tests, but
    with mixed fortunes: he tended, perhaps, to make less of
    his ability when opening than he might have done.

5. Bill Edrich, having failed in his first eight Tests, scored 219 in the fourth innings in the Timeless Test at Durban in 1939, when England, set 696 to win, scored 654 for 5. Edrich was not selected for any of the three Tests in England in the following summer, and played his next game for England in the third Test of the 1946 summer.

6. Alf Valentine and Sonny Ramadhin, playing for the West Indies against England at Trent Bridge in 1950, bowled 101.4 overs on the fourth day while England took their score from 87 for four to 350 for five. The West Indies bowled 145.4 overs altogether that day – this was only possible because Ramadhin and Valentine each got through a maiden over in about 95 seconds!

7. This occurred in 1926, when England trailed by 22 runs in the first innings of the fifth and decisive Test, the first four having been drawn. On a rain-affected wicket, Hobbs scored 100 and Sutcliffe 161, and England won decisively.

8. In the fifth Test at the Oval in 1968, Australia were set to make 352 to win. They soon fell into trouble and had only a draw to play for when heavy rain fell and seemed to have ended the game. However, the rain stopped and the groundsman asked for volunteers to mop up the ground; one wonders if he would have done so if it had been England playing for a draw. Play was resumed with 75 minutes remaining and five Australian wickets standing. Forty minutes went by before d'Oliveira took the first wicket, and then Underwood finished the match by taking four wickets in 27 balls.

9. Not the 1981 series, but that of 1954–55, when Australia collapsed before Tyson and Statham in the third Test at Melbourne and lost by 128 runs.

10. This was the classic final Test at the Oval in 1979, when England scored 305 and 334 for 8 declared, and India, having been out for 202 in the first innings, came very close to their target. Gavaskar's 221 was at the time a record for India against England.

40. Cricket books

1. *Back to the Mark* by Dennis Lillee, in which the fast bowler writes: 'I try to hit a batsman in the rib-cage when I bowl a purposeful bouncer.' This was written by Lillee (or his collaborator, Ian Brayshaw) in mid-career, and we may have to wait some time to know whether it was a part of his campaign to impose his will on batsmen, but I believe it was an honest description of what nearly all fast bowlers believe – that it is their right to use their speed to intimidate.

2. *Long Innings* by Sir Pelham Warner of Oxford, Middlesex and England. In the book he describes his tours to Australia, the West Indies, South Africa, Portugal, Denmark, the USA, etc.

3. *Fred* by John Arlott. A book which gets to the heart of its subject in a way that few cricketing biographies have equalled. I rate it as Arlott's best book, closely followed by his short biography of Maurice Tate.

4. *A Summer to Remember*, pictures by Patrick Eagar, narrative by Alan Ross, about the 1981 season. Eagar, son of the former Hampshire captain, is a most brilliant photographer, technically highly skilled and knowing enough about cricket to seize the vital moment to take his picture. Ross wrote four excellent tour books between 1955 and 1963 and then wrote very little more on cricket until he collaborated in this book. I very much hope that he will now write much, much more.

5. *On Top Down Under* by Ray Robinson. One of Australia's two best cricket writers (the other being the late Jack Fingleton) found a theme worthy of him, and every short biography is a small gem.

6. *Four Chukkas to Australia* by Jack Fingleton. The point is that a chukka is a period of play in polo and that Australia won the 1958–59 series, which the book describes, by four Tests to nil. The series was marred by controversy about the styles of the Australian bowlers, four of whom were generally thought of by the English press and players as 'chuckers'.

7. *From a Window at Lord's* by E. H. D. Sewell. Sewell, a former county cricketer, was an outspoken critic of the contemporary game in the 'twenties, 'thirties and 'forties. He wrote this book about the 1936–37 series in Australia from other people's accounts of the play, and without stirring outside England. I don't know whether the book sold, but the experiment has not been repeated.

8. *Beyond a Boundary* by C. L. R. James, which has a great deal to say about West Indian domestic cricket and politics. James' attitude to the game, and to his own book, is summed up in his paraphrase of Kipling, 'What do they know of cricket, who only cricket know?'

9. *Sing All a Green Willow* by Ronald Mason, one of my favourite writers. He has an excellent essay on the poet Francis Thompson and his poem about 'My Hornby and my Barlow long ago', and the piece on one Frederick J. Hyland, who played in just one first-class match which was virtually rained off, is brilliant.

10. *The Test Match Surprise*, allegedly by Jack Hobbs, describes a fictional Test series taking place in or around 1926, with the hero's love-story thrown in as a bonus. It is not at all clear who actually wrote it – Hobbs certainly did not, though it bears his name. It is quite hard to come by today, but Mason has an excellent account of it in *Sing All a Green Willow*, already mentioned in the answer to question 9.

Picture Quiz

1. Asif Iqbal, who set the ninth-wicket record of 190 with Intikhab Alam, against England at the Oval in 1967. Note the youthful Mike Brearley at slip.
2. This picture is of the Old England side taking the field against Surrey at the Oval in 1946. From left to right, the players are A. Sandham, E. Hendren, A. P. Freeman, M. W. Tate, M. J. C. Allom and P. G. H. Fender.
3. D. L. Underwood, England's most-used night-watchman, and E. D. Solkar (India).
4. The batting side get five runs (to the batsman, or byes or leg-byes, depending on the circumstances). David Gower hit the helmet off a bottom edge in the Centenary Test of 1980.
5. This picture was taken at Taunton when Jack Hobbs equalled W. G. Grace's record of 126 centuries in 1925. Hobbs raised his glass to the crowd; the drinks had been brought out by his captain, P. G. H. Fender.
6. This is D. J. Insole, who toured South Africa in 1956–57, playing in all five Tests, and played in one Test in each of 1950, 1955, 1956 and 1957.
7. C. I. J. Smith, otherwise known as 'Big Jim', who opened the batting with K. Farnes in the first Test of the 1934–35 series, at Bridgetown; they had already opened the bowling. Smith made a 'pair' in this, his first Test match.
8. Roy Marshall of the West Indies and Hampshire, who played his only Tests on the 1951–52 tour of Australia and New Zealand, and scored some 33,419 runs thereafter.
9. Alan Jones of Glamorgan who scored 1000 runs in a season for the twenty-second consecutive year. Two others have scored 1000 in more consecutive seasons in which first-class cricket was played, but with an inter-ruption caused by a war – Frank Woolley (1907–14 and 1919–38) and Philip Mead (1906–14 and 1919–36).
10. The batsman is F. J. Titmus, who missed 62 Tests between his forty-ninth match, in 1967–68 and his fiftieth, in 1974–75. The wicket-keeper is D. T. Lindsay of South Africa.